CHATHAM HALL

CHATHAM HALL

A History of Excellence

William Priestley Black

The History Press

Published by The History Press
Charleston, SC 29403
www.historypress.net

Front cover, lower: Photo by Robert Allen Ankrom.
All other cover images courtesy of the Chatham Hall Archive.

Unless otherwise noted, all images appear courtesy of the Chatham Hall Archive.

First published 2014

Manufactured in the United States

ISBN 978.1.62619.390.1

Library of Congress CIP data applied for.

This history of Chatham Hall is dedicated to the teachers, who for 120 years have built this school in their own way, sometimes with sacrifice, but always with dedication, joy and love. Their presence is quietly behind each of the chapters. Just as quietly, the history of Chatham Hall is their story, too.

Contents

Prologue

During my first year as a new faculty member at Chatham Hall, it was my custom to sit on the left side of the chapel facing the altar. Mandatory chapel was new to me, but as a conscientious guardian of unfamiliar rules, I wanted to observe my students and advisees to make certain they were fulfilling their obligation. My advisees were also creatures of habit, so that spot was a good place to observe their faithfulness.

I don't know when it was that I began to realize that each girl entering the chapel was a different person than the girl I was teaching. Each was also a different person from the one participating in an activity I chaperoned and different again from the girl on the athletic field. My own high school education had been in a mid-sized public high school. The boarding tradition was foreign to me, so my epiphany was more a shock of recognition that as an educator, I was seeing my students as complete people for the first time in my career.

Now after 30 years at Chatham Hall, it is my privilege to offer a vision of its history that I hope blends personalities and events into a unit that represents all the girls and all the adults who have given this school its personality. The framework of this vision moves through the tenures of each suceeding head of the school. There have only been fourteen in 120 years. Their administrations provide the background, but it is the people who tell the story. There have been brilliant shining moments; there have also been near disasters when it seemed that only divine intervention would save the school. Phoenix-like, Chatham Hall has always risen from the ashes of its own frightening moments to excel again and again.

Schools, by their very nature, belong to those in the present. Faculty and administrators plan for the future. Students benefit from the current excellence. Dusty old yearbooks and files of records are worth an interested glimpse of history from time to time, but what comes next is always more important.

Chatham Hall has been better than most schools in trying to preserve its history. Still, much has simply been lost. The disastrous fire of 1906 wiped out any local record of the founding and the first years. I have found information about these early years in some interesting places. I am grateful to the Archive of the Episcopal Church in Austin, Texas, and the Diocesan Office of the Diocese of Southern Virginia in Norfolk, Virginia, for records related to the first years. The Library of Virginia and the Virginia Historical Society in Richmond, Virginia, provided information that added to this view. I am grateful to the Jones Memorial Library of Lynchburg, Virginia, and the Danville, Virginia Public Library for help in piecing together the stories of Mrs. Willis and Dr. Lee. The Archive of the Presbyterian Church in Montreat, North Carolina, provided a glimpse of a sad moment for the school. Finally, I am grateful to alumnae and friends of Chatham Hall who have sent letters, pictures and stories.

Portions of this history appeared in serial fashion in *Chat*, published by the Chatham Hall Alumnae Association. The story of the 1970s to the centennial celebration appears here for the first time. In several instances, the earlier chapters have been revised with new discoveries. I am grateful to the alumnae association and to the board of trustees of Chatham Hall for their encouragement to publish this history.

I hope you will agree that this vision is one of courage, tenacity and a sacred trust well maintained.

Chapter 1

An Iris from the Widow Gilmer's Garden

The Chatham Female Episcopal School had only been in operation for five months when the executive committee of its board of trustees mailed out a printed appeal called a broadside seeking contributions for a new building. Signed by C.O. Pruden and Chiswell Dabney of Chatham and N.H. Massie of Danville, this broadside tells much about the origins of the school that was to evolve into Chatham Hall.

In part, the broadside is interesting as an announcement of the new school. Calling it a "rash undertaking considering our surroundings," the broadside proudly claims that the $3,000 raised locally would be sufficient to see it through its first year. In 1894, that $3,000 would have been approximately the equivalent of $81,000 in 2014 dollars, a significant amount of money for a small community to raise. Of even greater interest is the fact that the broadside claims that the new school's current location in a "rented house" cannot "accommodate applicants for the ensuing session." Unable to find a house in Chatham large enough, the board of trustees had determined that a new building would be "absolutely necessary." Apparently, the new Chatham Female Episcopal School was in great demand.

Equally important in the broadside are the grounds given by the executive committee for such an extraordinary appeal. After pointing out that the board of trustees is not "running it to make money," the broadside outlines the purpose of the school. "Our purpose," the broadside states, "is to establish a school in which a young lady can obtain a classical education at the minimum cost." Clearly, the trustees of the Chatham Female Episcopal School did not trust the fledgling public schools to do this.

The time was perfect for some dramatic changes in church schools in Virginia. The old Diocese of Virginia that had governed Virginia's Episcopal Church from its origins in the Jamestown Colony had just divided. All of southern Virginia had become the Diocese of Southern Virginia in 1892. The original diocese had maintained two boarding schools: Episcopal High School in Alexandria for boys and the Episcopal Female Institute in Staunton for girls. With the 1892 division, three of four educational institutions maintained by Virginia's Episcopal Church were geographically in the northern diocese. The new Diocese of Southern Virginia had pledged to share the support for all four schools, but it is clear there were misgivings about supporting schools that were of greater benefit to the northern diocese.

The appeal for funds to build a Chatham Female Episcopal Institute suggests that both the Alexandria and Staunton schools were distant and expensive. Calling the new Chatham Female Episcopal School a "need long felt," the signers of the broadside point out that "the majority of people entering our church in this section are of very small means" and note that these people "are not able to send their daughters to expensive church schools."

The Chatham Episcopal Female School had opened in September 1894, with thirty-five students, seven of whom were boarders, but its origins lie in a resolution passed by the Danville Convocation of the new Diocese of Southern Virginia in October 1892, just after the establishment of the Diocese of Southern Virginia. In pledging to share the support of education, the new diocese was taking on a women's college in Winchester and the Virginia Theological Seminary in Alexandria, in addition to the high schools in Staunton and Alexandria. Of the four, only the Episcopal Female Institute in Staunton was geographically in the new southern diocese.

Delegates to the Danville Convocation were clearly aware of the geography of the schools they had pledged to support. Although the minutes of the Danville Convocation are polite, there had apparently been a heated discussion regarding at least the high schools. Clevius Orlando Pruden, rector of Emmanuel Episcopal Church in Chatham, proposed that the new diocese establish its own high schools, a proposal seconded by Chiswell Dabney, a Chatham lawyer and vestryman of Pruden's church. The proposal might have passed had there been sufficient money, but funds were limited, and so it failed. However, delegates to the convocation endorsed Pruden's idea and authorized the establishment of both a boys' high school and a girls' high school—as long as neither would ask for diocesan financial support.

The Reverend Clevius Orlando Pruden.

Two Episcopal high schools were established as a result of the Danville Convocation of 1892. Those interested in establishing the girls' school in Chatham became its board of trustees; the Reverend C. Orlando Pruden became its president. Thirty-seven years old at the time, Pruden was the rector of Chatham's small parish with responsibility for four other neighboring churches. Born in 1856, Clevius Orlando Pruden was the seventh son of an important Nansemond County farming family. He had come to Chatham in 1884, to work with the Chatham Episcopal congregation during the Virginia Theological Seminary summer recess. Church members had liked him so much that they petitioned for him to return as the rector of Emmanuel Episcopal Church as soon as he had been ordained a priest.

As president of the board of trustees, C. Orlando Pruden had to secure independent funding for the new school, find a suitable location, apply to the Commonwealth of Virginia for a charter and find a suitable staff. Initially, money came from members of the Emmanuel Episcopal Church congregation and those Pruden called "non-communicant local Christians." The General Assembly considered the application for a charter during its 1893–94 session, approving the incorporation of the Chatham Female Episcopal Institute on February 24, 1894.

While raising funds and securing a charter, Pruden found a suitable building for the new school. The building was the family home of John Gilmer, situated on a hill directly to the east of the town of Chatham. A large frame house, named "Chatham Hall" by the Gilmer family, it stood at the crest of the hill overlooking Tanyard Creek, the town's eastern boundary. One of the area's most respected dairymen, John Gilmer had died suddenly in January 1894. Perhaps it was providential that C. Orlando Pruden was the executor of John Gilmer's estate. Whatever transpired, the widow Gilmer rented the home named "Chatham Hall"

The house in front of the taller frame structure is the original home of the widow Gilmer named "Chatham Hall," taken about 1898.

to house the school and continued to live there with her daughter for the next several years.

Chatham Hall was a large, white frame two-story building flanked by tall chimneys. Maude Carter Clement, one of the first graduates of Chatham Episcopal Institute, the name Chatham Female Institute assumed after one year of operation, wrote a personal recollection of this house in *The Early Homes of Chatham*, published in 1957. A third story tucked under its high-pitched tin roof would be converted into dormitory space. Perhaps the most distinctive feature of the house was a broad front porch that overlooked the town of Chatham. Its fancy scrolls and latticework are clearly visible in the few remaining early photographs of the school. Its formal dining room, a first-floor parlor and a study became the first classrooms. Bedrooms on the second floor were converted to accommodate the remaining Gilmer family, a headmistress, four teachers and seven boarders. The one-hundred-acre Gilmer dairy farm, named the Chatham Hall Dairy, would eventually provide most of the provisions the school would need.

Chatham Female Episcopal School opened in September with a headmistress, four teachers and thirty-five girls. The trustees had appointed Miss Jenny Nelson of Hanover, Virginia, as the first principal. Pruden reported to the diocese that Miss Nelson was a "lady of some years" who

The number of students shown in this circa 1895 photograph matches the reported 1894 enrollment. The woman to the right is probably Miss Jenny Nelson.

had experience with other girls' boarding academies in Virginia. She had graduated from the girls' high school in Staunton but had never received a formal university education. Even so, she was renowned as "the most perfectly educated woman in Virginia," known to have read the New Testament in both ancient Greek and Latin. Miss Nelson had taught French and classical languages at Wellesley College, chairing its language department for several of those years before coming to Chatham.

C. Orlando Pruden remained president of the board of trustees, as well as rector of Emmanuel Church. He would only head the school for a few months in 1900 as an "interim principal," but he would teach the required Bible course as rector of Emmanuel Church. The school had three divisions: Collegiate, Intermediate and Primary. Miss Nelson taught modern languages, Latin, history, literature and "Mental and Moral Sciences." Miss Neva O. Saunders taught mathematics, physics, physiology, chemistry and natural science. Miss Mary Gilmer, the widow Gilmer's daughter, taught art, physical culture, embroidery and elocution. Miss Isla Ragsdale taught typewriting and stenography.

In the spring of 1895, Miss Nelson decided that a "proper" school ought to have a literary magazine, so she assigned several articles. Isabelle Gilmer wrote a review of a Sir Walter Scott novel. Another put into verse the history of the Merovingian line of French kings. Other girls typed what had been written, and all was bound into a "magazine." Miss Gilmer, the art teacher, painted a cover for this magazine, a cluster of irises she had seen growing in the garden outside the former dining room. The colors were purple and gold, so the girls bound their "magazine" with purple and gold ribbon. Writing later about the final product, Maude Carter Clement stated that the girls were so delighted with the result that they started to wear purple and gold ribbons on their dresses as the school colors and adopted the name "iris" for the magazine.

Miss Nelson immediately set high standards for Chatham Female Episcopal School. She based the curriculum on the entrance requirements for Wellesley College. It is interesting that such modern business skills as typewriting and stenography were also included. The Primary Division underscores the weakness of education for young women at the end of the nineteenth century. Those accepted for this program only had to be able to write a simple sentence, read a simple passage, solve simple mathematical problems and know basic geography. Graduating in 1896, Rebecca Martin would be the new school's first and only graduate. When two more girls received their diplomas in 1898, the Chatham Female Episcopal Institute had become the Chatham Episcopal Institute.

Chapter 2

Purple and Gold

The 1898–99 session catalogue describes Chatham Episcopal Institute (CEI) as having been founded to "educate girls according to the best methods, along church lines, and at actual cost." The phrase "church lines" is further emphasized in referring to CEI as a "labor of love on the part of the Danville Convocation," as well as the board of trustees. Clearly, the convocation saw its school as a religious institution. While acknowledging that the convocation and the board of trustees may have given "their means to its establishment," the catalogue makes a far more parochial pronouncement in stating that CEI "is based on faith in Him who ministers to and blesses all efforts made for His people," as well as those who "uphold such an effort." Both the Chatham Episcopal Institute and the new Halifax Episcopal Male Academy were the result of what the catalogue deemed "rapid growth" in the Danville area of the diocese that had prompted a corresponding need for "intelligent, moral, and religious" education.

Clevius Orlando Pruden would remain president of the board of trustees until 1918 and a trustee until his death in 1921. As Pruden was rector of Emmanuel Episcopal Church in Chatham, the convocation also named him as the "rector in charge" of the school's religious life and education, making his a dual role until 1918. Pruden and the board of trustees handled financial matters, with Chiswell Dabney acting as treasurer. Pruden and the Danville Convocation influenced religious life and education. Day-to-day leadership of the school and its academic program fell to a lay principal.

By the time Richard Henry Willis arrived in the summer of 1898 to replace Jennie Nelson as principal, the school not only had a new name, the Chatham Episcopal Institute, having dropped the word "Female" from the name, but it had also expanded into two new wings, with a third wing under construction. There had been improvements to creature comfort, including the school's first "heating apparatus" for the main hall. The gift of a "valuable apparatus for scientific experiments in Chemistry and Physics" by Mr. George P. Terry of Mecklenburg County now enhanced academics. Best of all, Pruden reported in his 1898 report to the diocese that a $150 scholarship—the total cost of tuition, room and board—had been donated by Mr. W.W. Winslow of Pennsylvania to aid a "needy, but enterprising girl from the mountains of Virginia and North Carolina." Alice Finney of Pittsylvania County, Virginia, received the school's first scholarship.

Chatham Episcopal Institute had been, in Pruden's words, "fortunate" in securing Richard H. Willis as principal. Having taught as a professor of English and modern foreign languages, Richard Henry Willis, like Jennie Nelson, had come to the school with university-level teaching experience. However, unlike Jennie Nelson's self-taught scholarship, Willis had earned distinguished academic credentials, including a bachelor's degree from the University of Virginia, three different master's degrees and a doctorate from Illinois Wesleyan University—five academic degrees in all. In addition, Willis had gained extensive training in both French and German while living in Europe. Another similarity shared by Nelson and Willis sheds light on the direction the board of trustees wanted the school to take. Like Jennie Nelson, Richard Willis could trace his lineage back to colonial Virginia. George II of England had granted the Willis ancestors extensive lands in Orange County; Nelson's great-grandfather had been one of the signers of the Declaration of Independence. Together, Nelson and Willis represented both a firm

Dr. Richard Henry Willis. *The University of Arkansas Archive.*

commitment to quality instruction that would attract scholars and also a genteel Virginia tradition.

Willis took over Pruden's task of reporting annually to the diocese. Although he lived only long enough to submit one report, that one reveals much about the state of the school. Willis describes a prospering school with forty-five students enrolled, eighteen of whom were boarders. In spite of a "small epidemic of German Measles," the girls were gaining an average of seven pounds, a fact Willis attributed in part to the "pure healthy air at 800 feet above sea level, and partly to the excellent fare provided by [the] housekeeper." There is also a description of the daily schedule. Boarding students arose no later than 7:00 a.m., returned to their rooms no later than 9:30 p.m. and were in bed by 10:00 p.m. Five to five and a half hours of recitation daily were complemented by two hours of supervised study hall every evening. Religious instruction was handled either by C. Orlando Pruden or the Reverend J. Cleveland Hall of Danville, who is referred to simply as a "Lecturer" in the catalogue. In addition to twenty minutes of daily prayer, girls also read the Bible aloud daily, generally from the Book of Genesis in the morning. Afternoons were reserved for "a part of the Bible less suited for recitation."

Interestingly, Chatham Episcopal Institute maintained a Primary Department for elementary students from the area, as well as boarding girls who needed to study basic skills. Its main curriculum fell into three divisions. A two-year Normal Course prepared girls to teach in the public schools, bypassing the need for a university education. There was also a two-year Business Course that offered such office skills as typewriting and stenography. Premier among the courses of study was the Literary Course, CEI's preparation for higher education. Girls following the Literary Course took a daunting array of literary, writing, history and mathematics classes, as well as Latin and either French or German. For those intrepid enough to go beyond the curriculum, there was also instruction in Ancient Greek, Anglo-Saxon, Elocution, Physical Culture and Expression.

Clearly, CEI had ambitious plans. With the purchase of the one-hundred-acre Gilmer property in 1898, Chatham Episcopal Institute shed its temporary image as tenant of the rented Gilmer home, instead assuming an aura of permanence. Under the Willis leadership, the number of boarding students nearly doubled during his first year, forcing the school to convert alcoves into bedrooms. As owner of the building, the board of trustees was able to add attractive amenities for boarders, such as bathrooms and a system of hot and cold running water to each floor. The purchase of musical instruments, desks, maps and charts enhanced academic instruction. Art supplies from New York City and new books for the library added to what C. Orlando Pruden reported as the "most successful, and in every particular…gratifying session of the school's life." Unfortunately, Richard Willis did not live to see the blossoming of the school. He died of acute pneumonia on New Year's Day 1900. C. Orlando Pruden acted as interim principal until June 1900, his only actual leadership of the CEI program.

Willis's replacement, William Clarkson Marshall, came to Chatham during the summer of 1900, from the Episcopal Female Institute in Winchester, the women's college maintained jointly by the Episcopal Diocese of Virginia and the Episcopal Diocese of Southern Virginia. Marshall remains a vague figure. Lyon G. Tyler writes about him in *Men of Mark in Virginia: Ideals of American Life*, but there is no accompanying photograph. Marshall had gone to the University of Virginia from the northern Virginia town of Markham, graduating in 1883 with a degree in German. In that respect, he would have been similar to the late Dr. Willis. Even his college-level teaching credentials are similar, having taught at Episcopal Female Institute from 1888 until 1900. Tyler's description of Marshall as an "excellent teacher and disciplinarian" is echoed in the class will of the CEI class of 1901, which leaves him "the pleasant duty of reading rules, and delivering lectures to the new girls [newly enrolled students]," adding also the bequest of "the musical sounds of all voices heard in the dead hours of night. Marshall's wife, Lucy Meredith, fared a bit better, being willed "the flower garden with all its lovely tea roses and lilac bushes."

It is noteworthy that all three of the heads of school between the founding in 1894 and 1902 were language scholars and teachers. All girls were required to take classical Latin and modern French each year of their program, no matter the level. The more ambitious student could also add German to her course of study. Such language study alone would have distinguished Chatham Episcopal Institute as a more modern, forward-thinking institution.

Now that the diocese owned the former Gilmer property, accommodations were added for fifty more students and what Pruden referred to as a "corps of teachers." The principal lived within the school with his family. Teachers and a "matron" in charge of the dormitory also lived on campus. At the opening of the 1900–01 session, there were finally more boarders than day students, fifty-two to forty-nine. That year, Pruden announced in his report to the diocese that CEI was thriving so well that even the indebtedness incurred when buying the property and adding the accommodations had been reduced to a point that it was "no longer a burden or source of danger."

The school year was a long one, beginning the second Wednesday in September and extending to the end of the first week of June with only a single day's holiday given at Thanksgiving, ten days at Christmas and two days at Easter. As a boarding school, governance was advertised as that of the Christian family in which "kindly feeling, respect, courtesy, and refinement shall so prevail as to render special discipline rare." Any student "persistently impatient of control or out of harmony with…requirements" would be asked to leave. The rules simply demanded "lady-like conduct" at all times, first to mold CEI pupils into "what daughters, wives, and mothers ought to be," second to cultivate "minds, hearts, and physical health," third to teach "refinements in manners" and finally to build an "earnest Christian character." To that end, the principal monitored letters addressed to girls, inspecting anything considered "unauthorized" before directing the correspondent to cease contact.

Boarding girls came to CEI with few personal possessions. As all girls attended Sunday services at Emmanuel Episcopal Church in Chatham, each girl was required to have a winter uniform of dark, navy blue serge and the cap of the institute. In warmer weather, girls donned a white piqué dress and a straw sailor hat. With daily prayer and weekly services, each girl brought her own Bible; Episcopalians were required to bring a prayer book. Approved personal possessions were limited. In addition to everyday dresses, girls also brought an umbrella, overshoes, one pair of sheets, one pair of blankets with a counterpane, one pair of pillowcases, towels, table napkins and a napkin ring. The number of sheets and pillowcases had to be doubled if a girl preferred sleeping in a single bed.

The curriculum under Marshall remained that which had been introduced by Richard H. Willis; it would remain so until the 1920s. The catalogue for the 1900–01 session promised to prepare students "with advanced standing" to "any of the leading colleges or universities of the United States," naming as examples Vassar, Wellesley and Bryn Mawr. Girls electing the Normal Course would receive "excellent preparation for teaching in the common schools or high schools of Virginia or elsewhere." Girls electing only the two-year program rather than the full four years would be prepared to teach in the common (elementary) schools. There are, in fact, frequent alumnae notes in the CEI literary magazine from graduates teaching in Virginia schools.

Interestingly, the 1900–01 CEI bulletin invites "a few younger boys of refined manners" to participate in the Preparatory Course. These had to be younger than fifteen years of age and "gentlemanly in every particular."

Gym class, 1906.

Even the catalogue of 1888–89 notes: "We receive a few *gentle, young* boys as day pupils." The brief presence of younger boys on campus remains a mystery. It may be noteworthy that both C. Orlando Pruden and Chiswell Dabney were trustees of the Halifax Episcopal Male Academy, which was also a high school. These male students may have been preparing for the boys' high school in Halifax.

There were three levels of instruction at CEI. As a course designed to instruct girls in the "common school branches of education," the Preparatory Course prepared girls for admission to the regular high school program. Both girls and boys applying for the Primary Course had to correctly read an easy passage, write simple yet correct sentences, work rapidly in simple arithmetic and be familiar with elementary geography. One of the surviving photographs of CEI shows a large number of girls on the front porch of the old Gilmer residence with a row of young boys seated on the ground in front of them. The photograph also includes one adult male, possibly William C. Marshall. As no photograph of Marshall is known to exist, it is tantalizing to speculate that this may be the only photograph of the third head of the school.

Students in all courses received daily recitation grades that were accumulated every four weeks. Interestingly, there were no semiannual

Students are gathered in front of the Gilmer House in this circa 1902 photograph. William Clarkson Marshall stands near the "Academy Boys."

examinations, as CEI considered them a "physical strain" on a girl's health. Examinations were held only at the completion of a topic. Certificates of graduation seem more collegiate than secondary. Those girls completing the Literary Course received the degree of bachelor of philosophy (BPh) while those completing the Normal Course received the degree of licentiate of instruction (LI). Girls enrolled in the two-year Normal Course or the Business Course received a certificate of graduation. Literary and Normal Course graduates who completed an additional year of Latin or mathematics or three years of Greek, German or French received a bachelor of arts (BA) degree. Indeed, both the students and the *Danville Register* frequently referred to CEI as "the College."

Chapter 3

Surviving the Unthinkable

William C. Marshall left after two years without seeming to have affected the direction of CEI, forcing the school to seek its fourth head in only in its eighth year. With Marshall returning instead to assume the presidency of Episcopal Female Institute in Winchester, the trustees made what has proved to have been a momentous decision regarding the leadership of Chatham Episcopal Institute. C. Orlando Pruden reported to the Diocese of Southern Virginia that the trustees had elected as principal Elizabeth May Willis, the widow of Richard Henry Willis. Known as either "Lizbeth" or "Libby" to her friends, Elizabeth May Willis had come to Chatham as a young wife and mother but, a year later, had taken over art instruction at CEI when Mary Gilmer left at the close of the 1898–99 session. She had remained in that position after her husband's untimely death.

For a fledgling school, there could not have been a more natural choice. Born Elizabeth May Hall in Homer, New York, Mrs. Willis was a "degree graduate" of Syracuse University, having studied in the School of Fine Arts. Graduating in 1885, she had gone directly to the University of Arkansas, where she first taught in its Art Department and later directed the Arts and Crafts Department of Arkansas Industrial University, a division of the university established in 1885 for female students. University-level art instruction was still experimental. Indeed, the University of Arkansas catalogue notes that its "systems of education are being remodeled to include the aim of learning 'to do' something as well as 'to know' something." Having studied at the prestigious New York Art Institute, Elizabeth May Willis was clearly

Mrs. Elizabeth May Willis.

capable of teaching art. Perhaps the most significant contribution Mrs. Willis made to art was her mentoring of one of her students, Georgia O'Keeffe (CEI class of 1905). Willis recognized O'Keeffe's potential and gave her free access to the school's art resources and even later encouraged her to attend art school. As an artist in later years, O'Keeffe would credit her mentor as a major influence in her life. The reports she signed as "L[ibbie] M[ay] Hall" demonstrate that she was a competent administrator as well as an excellent art teacher.

As the widowed mother of two children—Richard Lee, born in 1893, and Katharine Murat, born in 1896—it is safe to assume that the board of trustees might have seen in Elizabeth May Willis an opportunity for stability in leadership that CEI had not yet enjoyed. She could be counted on to carry out the CEI program, essentially the work of her late husband. But Elizabeth May Willis did not fit the Virginia pattern. She was a native of Homer, New York, and a graduate of northern schools. If there had been any concern for these matters, any record of them has been lost. As the fourth head of the school, Elizabeth May Willis would be the first head to provide consistent leadership over an extended period of time. She directed the school's program for eighteen years, during which time she was strongly influential in shepherding the school through its first major crisis and later was a decisive influence in building a reputation for excellence.

Pruden marked the tenth anniversary of Chatham Episcopal Institute with an extensive report to the Diocese of Southern Virginia. In his 1904 report to the diocese, he noted that the tenth session had opened with 76 girls, 67 of whom were from Virginia. Since 1894, 672 had matriculated, but only 36 had graduated. With no debt remaining, the trustees were looking to building a large brick annex that would currently form a south wing and eventually anchor "a large handsome and up-to-date school plant with a capacity for one hundred and fifty boarding pupils." But the diocese still

Students gather on the front porch of the Gilmer House, spring 1905. Georgia O'Keeffe (CEI 1905) is seated at the top left.

did not support CEI financially. Its "diocesan school for girls" remained the Episcopal Female Institute in Staunton. Apparently referring to the group from the Danville Convocation that had begun the school in 1894, Pruden commented in his report that "we see the wisdom and opportunity for great usefulness in our aim in establishing and operating this school to furnish genuine and thorough education at the least possible cost."

By 1904, that cost had risen to $200 annually. Bishop Alfred Magill Randolph added his observations on the school in his address to the diocese. Beginning with a reference to a prominent Virginia educator who had been pleased with his daughter's "solid progress" at CEI, Bishop Randolph noted that the school was under "the sweetest Christian influences." One year earlier, Bishop Randolph had commented that the school had gained the confidence "of many of our most refined people throughout this and other states." Now he observed that "girls of the most refined families" were under the care of CEI.

The new brick annex did not materialize. The fact that CEI had outgrown its buildings led the trustees to add a northern frame annex that was ready for students when the school opened for the 1905–06 session. Now Chatham

Episcopal Institute was a rambling collection of three-story, rectangular frame buildings that stretched along the top of Gilmer's Hill overlooking the town of Chatham. Two of these were behind the original Gilmer home, one aligned on a north–south axis directly behind the original home, and one built at right angles to this wing. A wing to the south and one to the north now complemented this central complex. In front was the original Gilmer home, Chatham Hall. Everything was white frame with green trim and black tin roofs.

With such a jumble of frame buildings, the danger of fire was never far from mind. Adding to the concern were the numerous wood stoves that provided heat in the winter and the oil lamps that were the only source of light throughout the school. Students frequently practiced fire drills. In addition to a watchman who made rounds at intervals checking stoves, flues and lamps, seniors acted as "marshalls," trained to handle any of the extinguishers located throughout the buildings. There were also escape ladders placed at intervals throughout the dormitory sections. Such precautions were necessary as the only real source of water was from the large wooden water tank perched atop a metal tower looming behind the newest addition. The town of Chatham did not yet have a public water system, nor did it boast a regular fire company. So each student learned her duty and her evacuation route should the unthinkable happen.

CEI as it appeared shortly before the 1906 fire. The frame building at the left is the newly completed wing where the fire started.

Daisy Grubb (CEI 1907) created this drawing of the 1906 fire.

On Friday, February 16, 1906, the unthinkable did happen. That evening, there was a George Washington's Birthday celebration called a "German" with music, dancing and refreshments in the dining room on the lower level behind the old Gilmer home. All the girls assembled, along with the entire faculty, each one dressed in "evening clothes," for the occasion was considered one of the important formal functions. But there was another reason for a party that evening. One of the recent graduates from the class of 1905 was expected, so the party, as far as the girls were concerned, was as much in her honor as it was for Washington. Perhaps it was fortunate that a wreck on the Southern Railway prevented the arrival of the guest of honor.

It remains unclear who discovered the fire, but when someone shouted the alarm, Mrs. Willis bolted up to investigate with the Latin teacher hurrying behind her. By the time they reached the second floor on the north side of the new wing, they found the whole north wall ablaze. The fire was within the wall, now forcing itself out at every opening. Seniors who had followed Mrs. Willis worked the available extinguishers and, along with Mrs. Willis, battled the swiftly advancing flames in what one student, Nadja Fitts (CEI class of 1907), called a "brave but fruitless contest." Seeing that the situation was hopeless, Mrs. Willis ordered immediate evacuation of the entire school.

On the lower level, students had been working with teachers to remove the desks from classrooms before flames moved from the north wing to the rest of the school. Miss Burke, a teacher, returned to her own room to salvage what she could. After hurriedly packing her trunk, she put on her hat, checked in a mirror to see if it was straight, stuck in four hat pins and then carried the trunk down two flights of stairs, tossing it away from the building as she reached the door.

Mary Edwards, a student, was not as fortunate. It was easy enough returning to her room, but there she found her wardrobe already on fire, so nothing could be salvaged. Escape was more problematic. As she ran back down the hall, oil lamps exploded around her, spreading even more fire. Even worse, when she reached the steps by a single plank, she found they had already collapsed in flames, leaving only banisters standing free. There was no choice but to slide down the banister before the flames got to it, too.

Outside, Miss Carrie Taliaferro, assistant to the principal, took roll. Thankfully, all were present, but the school was lost. As some wrung their hands in despair, others searched through the piles of salvaged items to find something of their own. With roofs a rolling sea of flame by now, the courthouse of Chatham was ringing its alarm and townspeople were streaming up the hill to help. According to the news accounts of the fire, kindly families led one hundred dazed and bedraggled girls to spend the night in Chatham homes.

The following day, the *Danville Register* trumpeted the news of the fire, declaring "unbounded admiration" for the "courage and calm resourcefulness" of C. Orlando Pruden and May Willis. In truth, Pruden had been away at the town of Elba (now Gretna) as a visiting clergyman, unaware of the fire until after it was over. The executive committee of the board of trustees met almost immediately the day following the fire, announcing for the Monday morning Danville newspaper that the school would rebuild in brick and stone without delay. Temporary quarters were secured in the "largest private residence" in Chatham so quickly that classes resumed Wednesday, only five days following the fire.

State senator James Whittle had built that large residence for his daughter Matoaka when she married William E. Sims of Mississippi. Interestingly, Whittle had retained the title, while he himself lived outside Chatham in his estate named "Eldon." Both William Sims and James Whittle had died in 1892, leaving the Widow Sims alone in the large estate. Again, a series of coincidences benefitted the school. Whittle's brother had been bishop of the Diocese of Virginia just before the 1892 division into two dioceses that had

CEI girls gather at the home of Matoaka Sims on Whittle Street, Chatham, which served as the temporary school from February 1906 until September 1907.

engendered the call for the creation of the school. C. Orlando Pruden was the executor of Whittle's estate. Sims had made so many political enemies in Virginia following the Civil War that he had retreated to Mississippi before his death. The executor of the estate offered CEI the use of the building free of charge.

The girls of CEI settled into their temporary campus on Whittle Street without much concern for the effort needed. Four other houses on the same street had also been secured to act as dormitories. More would be built by local speculators who offered the houses for dormitories that would later be sold as homes. Most of these still stand in Chatham. The Sims House was the center of life and education. Girls attended classes and ate their meals there. In his own memoir of those years, a Chatham judge recalled how boys would sneak down to spy on the CEI girls playing basketball on their temporary athletic field. One student, Nadja Fitts, wrote in her history of the class of 1907 that girls had quickly substituted what she

Dormitory cottages built on Whittle Street later became family homes.

called "trials and tribulations" of fleeing flames for trigonometry, a "more dangerous foe."

Newspaper accounts during the spring months that followed the fire depict a school that was very much alive. Recitals had always been held in the Chatham Opera House, actually a large single room over stores on the town's main street. Three weeks following the fire, girls performed "A Tour Around the World" for the public. They set up booths in the style of Turkey, Japan, Switzerland, Alaska and Italy and performed a minuet in the area left open in the center. Throughout the spring of 1906, newspaper interest in CEI remained high because of the fire. Closing exercises that year were partly held in the same opera house. Music students performed, with each number "rendered in a most credible manner," and each graduate acquitted herself "with much honor." In addition to a demonstration of "free standing exercises" by the Physical Department, there was also a presentation of *A Midsummer Night's Dream*. As part of the closing festivities, the Art Department gave a studio tea, giving the public, according to the *Danville Register*, "the rare opportunity of feasting their eyes on numerous pieces of beautiful work."

Commencement activities stretched out over the weekend with a baccalaureate service at Emmanuel Church, with the Reverend W.A. Goodwin, rector of Bruton Parish Church in Williamsburg, delivering the sermon. Goodwin again spoke at the final commencement exercises on

Tuesday, speaking on a woman's influence as a power for good if founded on true character. Aside from the fact that this graduation is significant in that it happened at all, it is also noteworthy that Chatham Episcopal Institute awarded its first college degrees, a bachelor of arts and bachelor of music, both to Anna Phelps. Following the awarding of medals of distinction, C. Orlando Pruden, rector of Emmanuel Church, closed with a benediction. By that afternoon, teachers and students alike had made their way to the Southern Railway station and were gone.

Chapter 4

A More Dangerous Foe

Rebuilding does not seem to have been questioned. The *Danville Register* of February 22, 1906, reported on its front page a "mass meeting" of the citizens of Chatham at the town hall to rally support for the construction. Significant support from the community in the form of of $3,600 in cash and pledges had come from that rally. The frame structures had been insured for $14,000. Unfortunately, the new wing, the one where the fire had begun, had been built with borrowed money, a debt that amounted to $5,600, including what had to be paid out to move to the Sims House. The artithmatic was simple. Local pledges and insurance gave the school a little over $10,000, after the expenses associated with moving to temporary quarters had been paid. The estimated cost of the new building was $40,000, later raised to $45,000. That left a daunting minimum of $30,000 to raise. Still, the board of trustees accepted plans for the new building on April 7, not quite two months following the fire, and hired L.S. Agnor and Sons of Lynchburg to build it.

Pruden and Chiswell Dabney, treasurer for CEI, shared the task of soliciting contributions, Pruden traveling north, Dabney south. The division of labor was a wise move. Closely related to General J.E.B. Stewart, Dabney had been Stewart's aide de camp and later a captain of a Confederate cavalry during the War Between the States. Highly respected as a veteran, Dabney was also directly related to prominent Virginia families, including Chiswell Dabney Langhorne, the Lynchburg railway tycoon.

Raising the money to pay construction already underway proved to be more difficult than had been optimistically envisioned. When the devastation

Above: Architect's conceptual drawing for the new "college."

Left: The Reverend Chiswell Dabney.

caused by the April 18, 1906 San Francisco earthquake diverted public philanthropy, Pruden wrote hopefully to industrialist Andrew Carnegie asking for the full $30,000. Photographs of the destruction accompanied Pruden's plea for the necessity of rebuilding a school so essential for what he termed the "unfortunate class of girls in the South" who were being educated "at the least possible cost." Bishop Alfred Magill of the Diocese of Southern Virginia was more pointed about the "unfortunate girls." He declared that in Virginia, "many hundreds of families of gentlebirth and training" had been reduced to "comparative poverty." Any hope for educating a daughter "beyond the meager and imperfect training of the common country school, is closed." Bishop Randolph had been eloquent, but by the time the trustees gathered to lay the cornerstone of the new building on November 6, there had been no reply from Carnegie.

There is an interesting notation in later records regarding the funding of the new building. Pruden borrowed $750 from his wife, Julia Whickham Old Pruden, on the same day as the laying of the cornerstone. Apparently, Pruden had decided to confront Andrew Carnegie directly. He wrote to Andrew Carnegie as president of the board of trustees from the St. Denis

Hotel in New York on November 23, 1906. After repeating the history of the fire, Pruden refers to other letters of support that accompanied his petition: letters from Nellie Minner of Chatham; Eliot A. Kebler, president of Colorado Fuel and Iron; Andrew Jackson Montague, ex-governor of Virginia; and current governor of Virginia Augustus Swanson. It is noteworthy that Pruden's letter downplays the parochial-sounding name of Chatham Episcopal Institute in two ways. First, Pruden called the Episcopal Church one of the "more ecumenical" of American churches. Second, he affirmed the school's independence from church governance. A final appeal for the "homeless girls" and the "good work" of the school prompted a response.

On November 27, 1906, four days later, James Bertram, Carnegie's private secretary, wrote to Pruden at the St. Denis. While cautioning Pruden that "such an institution as the Chatham Episcopal Institute is not in Mr. Carnegie's field work," he nonetheless suggested that Carnegie sometimes allowed an exception and so asked for a statement showing what the school had before the fire, including all assets, and what was lost in the fire.

Pruden's list of assets and losses sent by return mail on November 28 underscores the extent of the emergency facing CEI. He estimates for Bertram that only $12,720.37 of value remained of what he estimated as having been $34,697.51 of value before the fire. Apparently Bertram was not satisified. Written in pencil on the reverse of the list is a list of questions asking for such specifics as assets before and after the fire, as well as the amount needed to make good the loss. At the end is the admonition, "It only wastes our time to use general expressions." Pruden's answer must have missed Bertram's demand for specifics, for on January 4, 1907, Bertram admonished Pruden that his lack of detail was putting him "to a great deal of trouble." The letter ends by repeating the warning that the school is "out of Mr. Carnegie's field."

Dealing with an industrialist and his private secretary was obviously difficult for Pruden. His letter of January 23, 1907, answering further questions exhibits a tone of weariness. One comment by Pruden suggests that there was an objection to the new buildings being more grand than the lost cluster of frame structures. "The erection of a more expensive house is unavoidable," Pruden wrote, adding "if we are to improve on the past." The building under construction in Chatham was "demanded by the times" and "worthy of the great work." Apparently, the answer was satisfactory. On March 5, 1907, Bertram noted that Mr. Carnegie had determined that the actual loss was $10,000 and that he would "gladly give you the last Five

Thousand dollars of the needed rebuilding fund…when you have had the rest contributed & expended."

With the new Chatham Episcopal Institute scheduled to open at the beginning of the 1907–08 academic year, Pruden and Dabney were facing their own "more dangerous foe." Raising $30,000 was proving difficult. The campaign to finance the new construction had slowed, but the builders were on schedule and expected to be paid for their work. The desperation is clear in Pruden's letters. Writing as president of the board of trustees on January 9, 1908, Pruden appealed to the Episcopal Board of Missions. The trustees had borrowed $15,000 from the Chatham Savings Bank to pay a remaining $22,500 construction debt, but the bank would not extend more credit. There was also a pledge of $7,000, but as it was promised "conditionally," Pruden was asking for $7,500 from the Men's Thank Offering. The school was unable to borrow any more and desperately needed to raise the $7,500 in order to meet a February 15, 1908 deadline. The situation was grave. "Unless we can secure this," Pruden wrote, "we are in great danger of most serious trouble."

Debt was the most dangerous foe for the first three years of the new building. By the first of January 1909, Pruden and the trustees had reduced the debt to $14,000, prompting Pruden to again appeal to Andrew Carnegie.

Reverend Pruden officiates at the laying of the cornerstone for the new CEI.

Writing directly to Carnegie himself rather than to James Bertram, Pruden hopefully asked for the full $10,000 Carnegie himself had determined was the actual fire loss. There was simply too much to raise before the final $5,000. With that money, Pruden was certain he and the trustees could raise the other $4,000 by that summer. After enumerating the reasons for the appeal and the difficulties he and the the trustees had encountered raising what they had, Pruden allowed a note of weariness to creep in when he wrote, "The strain has been so long and has become so constant and trying that I often fear that at any moment there may be a complete break down of my whole being." Pruden even suggests that the necessary exposure to a harsher, colder climate than was his custom had caused damage that could not be cured.

There was no positive response from Carnegie; Pruden and the trustees had to turn to other resources. On March 5, 1910, Pruden wrote to Carnegie that the school's trustees had "reached the conditions of the gift promised." Apparently, this letter was insufficient evidence that the conditions had been met. A sworn affidavit had to be secured before the final check would be sent. Acknowledgement of this final $5,000 was sent by Pruden with a cover letter to James Bertram on March 31, 1910. His letter concludes with thanks to Bertram and Carnegie on behalf of the 111 students at CEI. The ordeal was over. An invitation to visit Chatham Episcopal Institute does not seem to have been accepted.

Chapter 5

Expanding the "College"

The new CEI was an imposing building. By the time the class of 1907 trooped over to the old campus to plant their class tree, the "magnificent" new building was already nearing completion. The class will for the class of 1907 notes wistfully that students in the future will be able to fight their difficult subjects with "electric globes," make candy on the radiators in their rooms, attend midnight feasts "by way of the elevator" and take their Easter drive with Dr. Pruden in an automobile rather than the horse-drawn wagon.

Surpassing anything else in the area, the new CEI became a major attraction that was depicted on numerous postcards. A handsome reception hall three stories below a domed inner well was trimmed in honey-colored oak woodwork and furnished with Mission-style furniture. The statue of Venus standing on a pedestal at the foot of a grand staircase complemented prints of such important sites from antiquity as the Coliseum of Rome to suggest the classical nature of the CEI education.

To the left of the entrance hall was a formally furnished drawing room with a fireplace where boarding students could entertain visitors. A short hall between the drawing room and a private dining room led to the school's main dining room. That space occupied the entire end of the building, save for a small area set off for the kitchen. Mrs. Willis and her family lived in the apartment to the right of the entrance hall at the front of the building. To the left were classrooms and the school's small library. Faculty members had apartments on the upper floors. Perhaps the most significant area was

Right: The new "college" photographed from midway up the hill of College Avenue, now Pruden Street.

Below: The entrance hall of the new CEI built over the original well.

the art studio on the third floor. Stretching across the entire end of the building and as wide as two rooms, it also rose into the attic with a loft area. Skylights provided ample sunlight to supplement the gas lamps. This "central" building was to have housed only classrooms. Without the other buildings, the classrooms on the upper floor were, out of necessity, converted into dormitory space.

While housed in temporary buildings on Whittle Street, CEI had actually shrunk to 110 students, evenly divided between boarding and non-boarding students. Now there was a need to add more space. The new building had

The drawing room, to the left when entering the main building.

The new library, to the right when entering the main building.

attracted such increased patronage that the trustees authorized a second building adjacent to the new CEI. Named "Dabney Hall" in honor of the faithful service of Chiswell Dabney, the new hall would house a gymnasium, a "commodious" auditorium and, most significantly, enough new dormitory spaces to double the school's boarding student capacity. Once again, raising

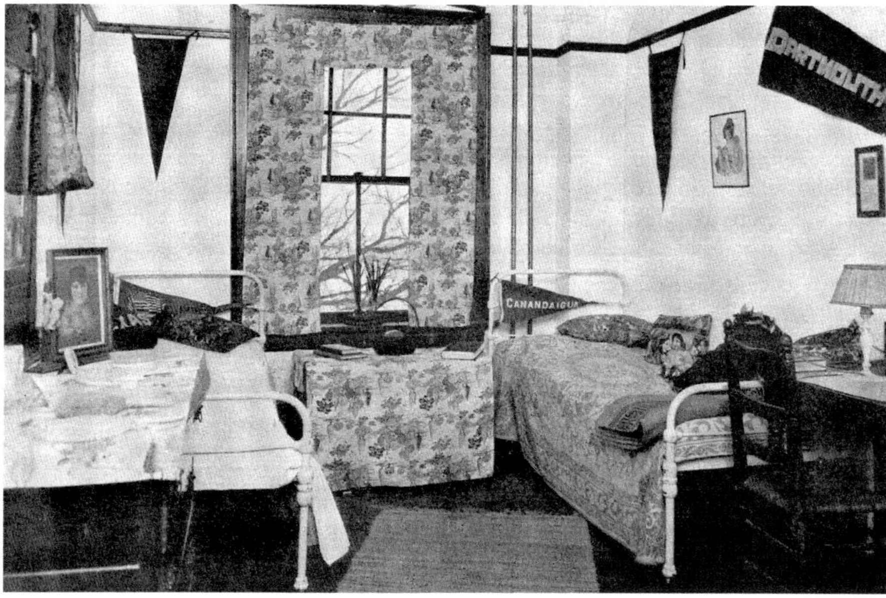

A typical dormitory room in Dabney Hall, pictured in 1912.

money for construction proved to be difficult. Only part of the building was completed by the initial opening on September 1, 1912. The southern section would have to wait.

The new CEI main building, now named in honor of C. Orlando Pruden, had been built at the top of the hill on the site of the original Gilmer mansion. Situated apart from the first building and farther down the southern slope, Dabney Hall had to include a significant basement level in order for its floors to be level with those of the Pruden Hall. Initially far less imposing than Pruden Hall, Dabney Hall was at first connected to the main building by a long, frame arcade. A steep flight of wooden steps in the front provided access until the southern portion of the building was completed in 1922 just after World War I and a more imposing pillared portico was added, enabling Dabney Hall to complement the Neoclassical style of Pruden Hall.

With Mrs. Willis and her family, as well as teachers, all having living quarters in Pruden Hall, Dabney Hall became the principal student residence. Its gymnasium on the basement level would pass through several transformations, but the main-level auditorium, a space that took up the entire north end of the main floor, would dominate the school's program for over half a century. It provided a central site for daily assemblies,

The dedication of Dabney Hall in 1911.

One half of the first floor of the new Dabney Hall was open space. Half of it was raked for an auditorium; the other half was level.

The lower level of Dabney Hall housed the first modern gymnasium.

entertainments, evening vesper services and evening study hall. As far as Sunday services were concerned, students would continue to walk into Chatham every Sunday to attend services at Emmanuel Episcopal Church, but they no longer had to use the Opera House over the Planters Bank on Chatham's Main Street for performances.

When a photographer recorded the burning of the school's mortgage on April 14, 1910, it was apparent that CEI had weathered a major financial crisis. Now the way was clear to embark on a new era of expansion. By the twentieth anniversary, the school seemed permanent enough to establish an alumnae association. Reverend Pruden wrote of the new association in a June 4, 1914 letter to Mrs. Robert H. Gregory of Wytheville, Virginia. After describing the recent commencement as "one of the very best," he announced the formation of an alumnae association by thirty-two students. "Every graduate will be written to & asked to join next commencement." Maude Carter Clement (CEI 1898) was the first president, Rose Hunt Womack (CEI 1907) was treasurer and Norma Cuthbert (CEI 1911) was secretary.

Five years later, as Chatham Episcopal Institute celebrated its twenty-fifth anniversary, changes in the Diocese of Southern Virginia provided new opportunities for governance of the school. In 1919, the diocese again divided, this time losing its western portion, a move that now placed all of

The burning of the mortgage on April 14, 1910.

Girls enter Emmanuel Episcopal Church on Main Street, Chatham, for the 1914 baccalaureate service.

The Riding Club, pictured in 1915.

the original diocesan schools, including the Female Institute in Staunton, outside the physical boundaries of the Diocese of Southern Virginia. Named Stuart Hall after 1912, the Staunton academy had become a financial drain for the diocese. In 1918, the bishop had made a special appeal to his diocese for $25,000 to help Stuart Hall relieve an "embarrassing debt" of $50,000. As a "labor of love" of the Danville Convocation of the Diocese of Southern Virginia, Chatham Episcopal Institute had already become the favored institution. Now there was a movement to divest the diocese of its obligation to Stuart Hall and make CEI its official diocesan school for girls.

By 1919, the Diocesan Committee on the State of the Church responded to the situation. After noting that "the division of the Diocese leaves us with but one institute of learning," the committee praised the action of the CEI board of trustees that had placed the school directly under "diocesan control." Indeed, Bishop Randolph praised CEI as a "Church School," calling the school "a monument to the zeal, the faith and the wisdom of the Rev. C.O. Pruden, D.D., its founder and president."

Although CEI had become the new "Diocesan School for Girls," there was little change in its financial fortunes. However, coming under the

Wagons taking girls on the nine-mile ride to the annual Galveston Mill picnic in May 1913.

CEI girls on the Galveston Mill waterwheel.

auspices of the diocese did raise issues of governance that would quickly come to a head. Since its founding, CEI had been governed by a board of trustees composed of local clergymen. Now that it was a diocesan school, Bishop Beverley Dandridge Tucker became the board's president, replacing Pruden, who had been president since the beginning. The Virginia Theological Seminary had conferred on Pruden an honorary doctor of divinity degree in recognition of these years of effort. Pruden, however, remained "Rector in Charge," a position that combined spiritual leadership with fiscal and physical oversight. Clearly, Pruden had done this since the very beginning. The school was the child of his imagination, and he had worked for twenty-five years, sometimes under exasperating circumstances, to build it. Apparently, he saw no reason for distinguishing between financial and physical matters and those matters of daily program that should have been the responsibility of the principal.

The distinction between areas of governance got its major test during the spring of 1920. In February, there had been reported cases of smallpox among the black population in Pittsylvania County, so students at CEI were inoculated against the disease and quarantined. That same February, a senior, Ann Harmon Cordell, wrote to her mother about the boredom and asked first if it was acceptable to play cards on Sunday and later described a game of chance she called "Filipino."

When Mrs. Willis later got wind of the games, she told students at the beginning of study hall that "Filipino" was actually a form of gambling and ordered everything that had been "won" returned. Apparently, Mrs. Willis also understood the boredom her girls had experienced and softened the "gambling" label by telling them that she had played the game as a little girl. At that, Pruden rose and begged to disagree, calling the game "plain gambling." When Mrs. Willis tried to explain her side, Pruden dismissed her explanation, starting what Ann Cordell described to her mother as an "argument right on the platform." Ann Cordell ended her letter dismissing Pruden as "the rudest old man," but she would soon have more serious matters to write about.

Sunday, February 25, brought a Sunday school lesson on Harriet Beecher Stowe. CEI had instituted a series of lessons from the Episcopal Church on "Heroes of Faith," focusing on persons from history who had "defied public opinion or scorn for the sake of history." Knowing that Stowe's *Uncle Tom's Cabin* was still controversial, Mrs. Willis considered the advisability of dropping the Stowe lesson. While seated with Dr. Pruden on the stage just before assembly, she privately told Dr. Pruden her opinion. Pruden, however,

A dorm room in Pruden Hall.

disagreed. Mrs. Willis suggested that the matter be put up for a student vote and indeed raised the issue, receiving an evenly split decision. Half were for the lesson; half voted against Stowe. According to a later account, Pruden "forestalled" Mrs. Willis and voiced his resentment that she would attempt to override his authority and gave "severe" public criticism of Mrs. Willis. As far as Ann Cordell was concerned, Dr. Pruden only wanted the lesson "because he likes to talk." Writing about the incident two months later, Chiswell Dabney observed that Pruden had wanted to "make some criticism on the work." Pruden's victory turned out to be costly.

On March 11, Ann Cordell wrote to her mother describing a second phase to the Harriet Beecher Stowe issue, saying, "We've just had the biggest scrap!" After reminding her mother of Pruden's having contradicted Mrs. Willis on the "Filipino" issue and the Sunday school lesson, she told her mother about the assembly she had just attended at which Pruden had explained his earlier remarks to the assembled students. According to Ann Cordell, Pruden got up in assembly and apologized for his manner but not the choice of Sunday school topic. Warming to his topic, Pruden then condemned Mrs. Willis for "overstepping her rights when she put the matter to a vote after his disapproval."

Calling the situation "terrible," Ann Cordell depicted Pruden as a man out of control. "He raved about his being the head of the school," Ann wrote, pointing out that he had also called Mrs. Willis "subordinate" to him. At the end of his speech, Pruden "just as good as impeached her [Mrs. Willis] before the whole student body and faculty."

Governance was the issue. As the man who had founded the school, scratched for its financial support and been intimately involved in its welfare, Pruden must have had a patriarchal attitude that would not tolerate what he interpreted as "insubordination." Even the *Danville Register* ultimately saw the friction between Willis and Pruden as a "question of whose authority in the school was supreme."

When Pruden finished and sat down, Mrs. Willis rose, "white as a sheet and *mad*" to address her students. Her comment at the assembly showed admirable control. Saying that she had never approved discussing private matters in public, she simply dismissed the incident, saying that she was "very sorry that has been done." But Ann Cordell's letter depicted a school in "confusion." Apparently, Mrs. Willis wished to defuse any anxiety by speaking to the students at lunch that day. Observing first that Dr. Pruden's speech was a great surprise, she "tried to smooth things over" by explaining that Dr. Pruden had thought she was trying to usurp his rights and had "brooded over it too much." To this report, Ann Cordell added her own observation that Pruden was "rather old" and suffering from high blood pressure.

Attempts to smooth things over failed. First, the faculty was furious. At least ten sent a letter to Dr. Pruden saying they disapproved of his "rudeness" and demanded a public apology. It is unclear who called the student body together, but Ann Cordell spoke of a student meeting where students voted to send a letter of support to Mrs. Willis.

Apparently, they were divided on the issue of sending a letter of protest to Dr. Pruden. The following morning, Mrs. Willis again addressed the students. She told them that she had been at the dentist and had not known of a student meeting and wanted the whole thing dropped. Later that day, Pruden also addressed the students again, telling them that the whole matter between principal and founder had been arranged "satisfactorily." Unfortunately, he did not let the matter rest. Instead, according to Ann Cordell, he continued to complain that he had not been "treated right by the faculty or the students."

Mrs. Willis's admonition that she never wanted the matter alluded to again evidently held for nearly a month, but on April 9, Ann Cordell shared the "bombshell" that ten teachers had resigned and were leaving the following week, almost two months before the end of the term. These included Ann's French, English, chemistry and civics teachers, CEI's oldest and best. These were the ones who had protested Pruden's rudeness to Mrs. Willis before the student body. Pruden's revenge for the letter of protest was a letter to each of the teachers that her services would not be required the next year. As a group, they replied to Dr. Pruden that if they were not required next year, they surely were not required now and offered their resignations. According to Ann, they said "that unless he acknowledged to them that his criticisms of Mrs. Willis had been wrong, they would go anyway."

At this point, the *Danville Register* learned of the situation and sent a staff writer to investigate. On Tuesday, April 27, the front page trumpeted:

Faculty Quit in Sympathy with Principal

The second line twists the matter, focusing on the Harriet Beecher Stowe lesson rather than the issue of governance and civility.

Trouble at CEI Outgrowth of Lecture on Mrs. Stowe

Initially, the *Danville Register* reported that Mrs. Willis had scheduled a lesson on *Uncle Tom's Cabin* that had been cancelled by Pruden out of sympathy for a school of southern girls. For this reporter, the trouble lay in the fact that Mrs. Willis, a northerner, had scheduled a speaker from the North. Those faculty members who sympathized with her were, themselves, graduates of New England or northern women's colleges who attributed Pruden's attitude to "prejudice or provincialism or ancient untra-conservativism." According to the story, Mrs. Willis had resigned in protest, and the other ladies had "me-too'd." CEI, puffed the reporter, was allied by its traditions with "southern ideas and views." Surely this was an "exemplification of 'When South meets North.'"

There is an element of truth in the assertion that the matter was in part north meeting south. As a young boy, Clevius Orlando Pruden had lived on a farm near Suffolk, Virginia, during the Civil War. The entire county, including the nearby town of Chucatuck, had remained largely a contested no-man's land throughout the war. Pruden would have experienced first the occupation of the area by Union troops for two years and the failed Confederate two-month-long siege of Suffolk. His unpleasant experiences would have been coupled by the agonizing Reconstruction. Surely he had something to say about Mrs. Stowe, but that memory was only part of the issue.

On April 30, the *Danville Register* continued to cling to its perception that the Harriet Beecher Stowe lesson was the root of the controversy. While the newspaper was myopic about the root of the issue, it was correct in its report that teachers were leaving. Even Bishop Beverley Dandridge Tucker, who had hurried from the diocesan office in Norfork, was unable to convince them to stay at least until the end of the term. His attempts to calm the situation failed. By May 1, Chiswell Dabney wrote to his daughter that "bitterness was so visible between parties" that no resolution would be possible. As a student, Ann Cordell fumed to her mother that the bishop could not get Pruden to admit that he was wrong. "Everyone always said he would ruin this school, and he certainly has done his darndest this year." At a hastily called meeting of the board of trustees, Pruden insisted that Mrs. Willis had to go, but the board was reluctant to have her "dismissed," especially, as Chiswell Dabney noted to his daughter, "in view of her long & valuable service." Instead, Dabney reported that the board ignored Pruden's demand that Mrs. Willis be dismissed and offered her the headship for the 1920–21 session. Sadly, the damage had been done. Mrs. Willis expressed her gratitude for "confidence" and "affirmation" but offered her resignation.

Half of the girls dressed as men for the Cotillion Club dances.

With the departure of ten of its most important teachers, CEI faced the final month of its 1919–20 session scrambling to find anyone who could continue instruction in those subject areas. With such short notice, many of the temporary teachers were either untrained or ill-suited for the boarding environment. Mrs. Willis apparently intended to remain until the end of the term but took a few days off to stay with her daughter, Katherine Murat, in Pennsylvania. A graduate of CEI, Katherine had even taught art for one year. Her wedding in the main entrance hall had been the first alumna wedding for the school. Those happier memories were even more shattered when she was killed in an automobile accident driving her mother to her home in Bala Cynwyd, Pennsylvania, from the railway station in Philadelphia. Mrs. Willis was so badly injured that she was unable to return to CEI for her final graduation.

Chapter 6

Reaching for a New Age

The board of trustees quickly hired Annie Marion Powell of Wytheville, Virginia, as the new principal. A graduate of Sweetbriar College with a master's of art from Columbia University, Miss Powell brought with her nine years of experience with boarding schools. C. Orlando Pruden referred to her in his report to the diocese as a "Virginia lady of high Christian character, wonderful tact and consecrated common sense." With 172 students enrolled at the opening of the 1920–21 session, Chatham Episcopal Institute emerged from the Willis-Pruden fracas without damaging enrollment, but the faculty was still unstable. None of the temporary faculty hired after the departure of the ten faculty members in April remained. Only three of those hired for the new session would stay more than one year.

CEI did have an $8,000 endowment, but it also had a troubling debt of $43,000 largely remaining from the construction of Dabney Hall. Depending on income from enrollment, CEI had to maintain its numbers. With that in mind, Pruden announced to the diocese in 1921 that the school was now planning to build another building, matching Dabney Hall, connected to the north side of Pruden Hall with an arcade that matched the one on the southern side connecting Dabney Hall. The three would have presented a handsome, unified row overlooking the town of Chatham. As chair of the board of trustees, Bishop Tucker excitedly referred to the school's financial needs, saying that "those who realize the value of the proper training of our young women" would surely find no stronger appeal.

Left: Miss Annie Marion Powell.

Below: Ambitious plans called for two dormitory buildings to flank a central classroom building. Only Dabney Hall to the south was built.

The proposed third building would never be built. Instead, the 1920s proved to be a period of conflicting fortunes for CEI rather than a period of growth. On the one hand, Annie Marion Powell would introduce what the yearbook labeled "progressive" changes in the curriculum and daily life of the school; opposed was a steady decline in enrollment that reflected a change in desire to enroll. As an institution that relied solely on income from tuition for its daily operation, the steady decline would be an increasing threat.

The Saturday, December 10 front page of the *Danville Register* reported in bold headlines the sudden death of C. Orlando Pruden. He and his wife, Julia, had been accustomed to visiting her family near Richmond at the end of each year. He had been stricken by a heart attack while he and his wife were dining with friends on Friday, December 9. Newspapers announced that the rector of Chatham's Emmanuel Episcopal Church would conduct a simple funeral, but by the time the train bearing Pruden's remains arrived in Chatham, the funeral had become, according to Chiswell Dabney, "such a funeral" as Chatham had never before seen. The Right Reverend Beverly Dandridge Tucker, bishop of the Diocese of Southern Virginia, officiated at the Sunday funeral. Four other clergymen assisted, with Chiswell Dabney taking a special place of honor as one of those who had worked with Pruden in establishing the school. Pallbearers were men from the town who had attended the CEI academy. One of them, Samuel Sours, had actually graduated as the school's sole male alumnus in the class of 1914. As the funeral cortege made its way to Chatham's old cemetery, CEI girls bore flowers they would lay on the grave.

Pruden's role in the founding of such an important institution was noted, but newspapers never forget a bit of controversy. At the end of one article, a reporter dredged up the dissention between Mrs. Willis and Dr. Pruden, referring to it as an "animated discussion on the question of permitting a lecture on the life and works of Harriet Beecher Stowe," adding the final observation that Dr. Pruden had taken a "pronounced stand."

As America emerged from World War I into the changing social and economic atmosphere of the 1920s, Chatham Episcopal Institute, too, began to experiment with such progressive innovations as student participation in the governance of the school. Mrs. Willis had instituted a student council in 1918 made up of one representative from each of the classes and a president, but its responsibility for upholding the "cherished honor rules of C.E.I." did not specify any designated duties. Miss Powell changed the student council in 1920 to a sixteen-member body with four representatives from each of the classes. These girls had responsibility for quiet hours and study hall. The introduction of a branch of the Girls' Friendly Society in 1921 prompted yet another change in student government.

The Girls' Friendly Society (GFS) added the important dimension of service to CEI. A junior auxiliary had stitched blankets and cloth dolls for mountain communities in western Virginia, but the GFS would expand the concept of service to the school as well. Founded in 1875 in England, the object of the society was "to uphold the Christian standards of honor and morality." Under the motto "Bear ye one another's burdens," the society promoted "friendship, purity, steadfastness, and religion." With each student a member, the CEI chapter of the Girls' Friendly Society was the largest in the world. It took on the responsibility for welcoming new girls with a party at the beginning of the year to promote a "friendly, tolerant" spirit at CEI. Service to the school included leading prayers on Wednesday and Sunday evenings. Service to the community included collecting Thanksgiving donations "for those in distress" and sewing clothes for the mountain people during Lent. At graduation, the GFS added a vesper service the Sunday evening prior to the Tuesday graduation. Almost immediately, the GFS became more important than the student government.

Reporting to the diocese after Pruden's death, Annie Marion Powell noted the need for "greater breadth" and a "larger vision" for CEI. The academic program was expanded with the 1923 transformation of the Dabney gym into a chemistry lab, the refitting of classrooms and the enlargement of the library on the first floor of Pruden Hall. Even so, the curriculum remained much as Richard Willis had created. However, the daily life of the school became more active. Miss Powell's observation that outdoor sports would be a draw for enrollment led to the construction of a swimming pool in 1927, as well as additional tennis courts and a four-hole golf course on the lawn in front of the two major buildings. Indeed, sports became a major element within the daily life of the school. An athletic board oversaw competition between classes in basketball, field hockey, track and tennis, pitting freshmen against sophomores and juniors against seniors. Honorary varsity teams were selected from among the best players. Other organizations such as the Dramatic, Art, Home Economics and French Clubs; an orchestra; and a day students' league called the "Hill Climbers" showed a quickening of energy in the school.

New ceremonies also became part of CEI under Miss Powell. Other schools were crowning "homecoming queens"; CEI crowned the Queen of May at a May Day celebration that had appeared first in 1915. Students voted for their queen. Others dressed in elaborate medieval or eighteenth-century costumes as members of the court. As the ceremony gained importance, dancers began to execute the elaborate maypole dance, and students wearing white dresses adorned with greenery would dance for the queen and her court. By 1924, the May Day celebration had become the event that drew alumnae for an annual Alumnae Luncheon. More enduring than

The field hockey team, pictured in 1925.

May Day was the change in graduation. Commencement activities began with a public recital given by music students, accompanied by an exhibition mounted by art students. Saturday was Class Day. Faculty members gave a formal tea for graduating seniors. The Expression Department treated the entire school to the spring play. Sunday service at Emmanuel Church was the baccalaureate sermon, followed that evening by the final vesper service of the year. In 1922, Miss Powell introduced a lantern ceremony following vespers that marked the passing of the school from the graduating class to the rising junior class. Actual commencement exercises were Tuesday morning. By late afternoon on Tuesday, all girls had found their way to the Southern Railway depot and were on their way home.

Unfortunately, CEI did not benefit from the expanding economy that brought the new prosperity of the 1920s. A rural financial depression that had followed the war made it more difficult for CEI to draw from its traditional constituency. Since 1894, CEI had served girls unable to get an education locally, but by 1922, Miss Powell was reporting to the diocese that improvement in Virginia public schools was making it unnecessary for families to even consider sending a daughter to boarding school. Numbers

The CEI May Court remained an elaborate local event that drew visitors to Chatham until World War II. It was never revived. Pictured is the 1915 May Court.

were declining. The 1920–21 session had opened with 143 boarding and 29 day students. By the 1922–23 session, that number had dropped almost 25 percent to 108 boarding and 35 day students. Clearly, Chatham Episcopal Institute needed to change its appeal from a school that catered to the educational needs of girls within the diocese. Although girls were enrolling from outside Virginia, the graduating senior classes would remain approximately half from nearby Virginia communities. The majority of out-of-state girls came from North Carolina, West Virginia, Maryland and the District of Columbia, with some representation from New York and New Jersey. Occasionally, an exotic Wisconsin, Florida, Delaware or Connecticut girl would slip in.

Annie Marion Powell left after the 1924–25 session to take over Stuart Hall in Stanton, having brought about changes in student life but not having stemmed the declining enrollment. Mabel Eleanor Stone assumed direction of the school that summer. Under her leadership, workmen leveled the floor of the auditorium, making that space appropriate for a large study hall as well as a commons room. Even if students may not have wanted a large study hall, the Cotillion Club, an organization in which half of the girls dressed as boys for a dance, now had a more appropriate space for dances. The club now moved from the main entrance hall of Pruden Hall to the commons area, where students could push desks aside to gain a large, open space. Mrs. Stone also experimented with student self-government. At first, seniors

Right: Miss Mabel Eleanor Stone.

Below: Housed in a frame structure behind Pruden Hall, the 1927 swimming pool was part of the expanded athletic program for more "modern" girls.

imposed on themselves what they called Mrs. Stone's "official edicts." These were seen by students as "liberal privileges." Clearly, Miss Stone's intent had been educational, but as a later head of the school would observe, the natural tendencies of human nature were not sufficiently safeguarded or controlled.

There was soon betrayal of Miss Stone's trust and, with that betrayal, an accompanying decline in discipline. This is evident in the 1927 yearbook, where a piracy theme depicts a fractious crew boasting of its exploits while the captain, Miss Stone, was "a-pacing the bridge." One claimed that "nary a one" had been caught playing cards half the night, while another crowed that she had smoked the whole time the captain was at lunch, although the "smell o' the weed" was prohibited. Humorously, the crew is discovered at the end of the essay, but the captain's response suggests an indulgence that would eventually damage the school. In the story, the captain tells the miscreants they must learn that the reason they "cannot have these treasures we so desire is because you try to get them alone and will not wait until we are all ready to get them together." Rather than ending with punishment, the story ends with forgiveness and understanding. The captain will "trust" once more if those involved would "swear not to break faith with me again."

In truth, the nautical theme of that yearbook was an apt one for the school. Attempting a more modern appeal, Chatham Episcopal Institute was jettisoning its old image as a church school like so much superfluous cargo from a sinking ship. Most significant among the changes was the name. By adopting Chatham Hall in lieu of Chatham Episcopal Institute, there might have been a broader appeal, a tactic that seemed to have worked for the Virginia Female Institute when it changed to Stuart Hall in 1912. Now the identity shifted back to the estate where Pruden had opened his school in 1894, thereby dropping the reference to the church ultimately responsible for it.

Efforts to stem the decline in enrollment failed. Judge Langhorne Jones of Chatham later wrote that the school's reputation had become so questioned that Hargrave Military Academy cadets would try to persuade their parents not to send their sisters to Chatham Hall. It seems that the former distance between the two schools had narrowed. One 1928 graduate of Chatham Hall reminisced that Hargrave cadets would get day students to deliver messages to boarding students setting up a clandestine rendezvous. Nancy Wooding (CH 1926) humorously observed the change.

"Chatham in the Stone Age"

The line was trudging up the hill
But where was all the flock?
Why surely not two-thirds were ill
Or fallen back a block.

I sat a while and waited
Expectant of some light;
And my patience was rewarded
By a most unusual sight.

The rest were slowly coming—
I was surprised, you bet—
For at the side of each fair one
Was an H.M.A. cadet.

Enrollment was hemorrhaging. Chatham Episcopal Institute had opened with 110 students for the 1926–27 session, with only the addition of 10 in a college class, a two-year advanced course that was the equivalent of a junior college. That number slipped to 90 the next year, with 7 in the college class. Just one year later, enrollment was 87, 16 of whom were college and 15 from a new seventh and eighth grade.

The Reverend Edmund Jennings Lee.

Acting as president of the board of trustees, Bishop Beverly Dandridge Tucker led the trustees to take drastic measures. Of primary importance was leadership. Tucker wrote to Edmund Jennings Lee, a distant cousin, inviting him to visit the school and consider becoming its principal. At the same time, Lee would be rector of Emmanuel Episcopal Church in Chatham, enabling him to be both the school's head and the "Rector in Charge" representing the diocesan trustees, a combination never before achieved. Financially, the school had to raise enough money to get out of debt and to ensure its future. To that end, the trustees hired a fundraising firm and launched a "Campaign for the School" with the slogan "Chatham Hall for Virginians and Virginians for Chatham Hall." Citing a goal of $325,000, the campaign seems to have limped rather than sprung into action with an apology that Chatham Hall had been "experiencing many difficulties." As it neither catered to the "economically and socially elect" nor had any form of endowment, the school simply needed help to survive.

Chapter 7

The Lees

Edmund Jennings Lee had been a missionary in Anking, China (now Anquing), for twenty-five years and had only been in America for a few months before he visited Chatham. His return had not been a happy one, as he had been displaced by the upheaval of civil war in China in April 1927. He had spent the previous years in charge of the evangelical work in the American Church Mission in Anking, but his work there had been as much administrative as it had been religious. He had been responsible for traveling by whatever means available to distant "outstation" mission groups often enduring hardship and discomfort. Especially important to Chatham Hall had been his experience with the founding of six mission schools, including a boys' boarding school and a girls' boarding school and significant work in founding the Kuling School, a boarding school for the children of expatriate Americans and Europeans. Also important was his experience raising funds for mission programs.

Apparently, Edmund Lee was not at first certain that he wanted the job. Even after escorting his family and mission personnel to the safety of Shanghai, Lee had wanted to return to his work. It was only after becoming gravely ill in May 1927 that he had to follow his family back to the United States. When contacted by Bishop Tucker, Lee had been lecturing on the situation in China. He loved China, felt strongly about his own mission and wanted to return. Writing in a circular letter to his friends in July 1928, Lee self-deprecatingly referred to his talents, saying that the trustees were more certain than he that his experience would qualify him to meet the needs of the school. Still, the school made an extremely strong appeal, and he finally "capitulated."

When Edmund and Lucy Lee arrived in Chatham in May 1928, the situation was even worse than it had been when Miss Stone resigned. The "Campaign for the School" had been such a disappointment that it was failing even to raise enough money to pay the firm hired to conduct it. By June 1928, there were only twelve students registered for the 1928–29 session, and the school had a debt of $30,000, much of it to suppliers that would not extend credit for the school to open again. By mid-June, the bishop and its new principal agreed with the other trustees that Chatham Hall was no longer able to continue, and so Lee began the necessary measures to close it down after thirty-four years.

Edmund Lee later wrote that his first step in closing down the school was to call in William Morrison, the headwaiter for the dining room. Morrison, who had been with the school since 1898, would be leaving the next day to work at a summer camp, and Lee wanted him to know that there was little chance of Chatham Hall's reopening in September. William Morrison surprised Lee. Rather than accepting the pronouncement that he had to look for a new job, he challenged Lee's faith in divine intervention. "This school was founded on faith and prayer," Morrison told Lee. "It will never close." His advice was simple: "When you get to a place where you don't know what to do nor where to turn, the good Lord will come out and fix things up for you." His parting comment was that God had taken care of the school in the past; that was the way it would be now.

With William Morrison's polite rebuke still on his mind, Lee joined Reverend Wicker, a trustee, for a trip to Lynchburg, where together they would make a final appeal for aid, this time to John W. Craddock, the founder of Craddock-Terry Shoe Company. The meeting might even be considered providential. Craddock had been given several hundred thousand dollars by Frank H. Kidder of Boston, Massachusetts, with the directive that he should distribute it among charities. Fortunately, Craddock had a connection to the founding of Chatham Hall, albeit a slender one, through his now deceased first wife, Mary Peachy Gilmer of Chatham. Her family had owned the house named Chatham Hall where Pruden had first housed the Chatham Episcopal Institute in 1894.

Edmund Lee returned to Chatham that night with $15,000 and immediately sent for William Morrison to tell him that his faith had been justified. However, recovering from the euphoria of this initial success, Lee came to the sobering realization that they could not "climb out of a $30,000 hole with a $15,000 ladder." With the zeal of a new convert, he immediately wrote to John Craddock asking for $5,000 more, half apologizing that he had been accused before of having "consecrated nerve." If Craddock should think Lee had too much nerve asking for an additional $5,000, Lee hoped Craddock would forgive the request as it was "consecrated." The letter worked. John Craddock replied that he was impressed with consecrated nerve and gave an additional $10,000, to which he later added a final $8,000.

With a total of $33,000, Lee was able to pay off the important debts and make preparations for the opening of school. There would be another significant gift that year that would enable Chatham Hall to survive the 1928–29 session: Mrs. Arthur Kelly Evans (Lettie Pate Whitehead Evans, 1895–1953) of Hot Springs, Virginia, gave $25,000. Still, there were few students, and many of the former faculty members had left, taking more assured jobs. During the remainder of the summer, Edmund Lee canvassed the state of Virginia speaking with clergymen and families about sending girls to Chatham Hall. At one point, one mother even thought he wanted her to enroll instead of her daughter, but his perseverance saved the school.

By opening day in September 1928, there were seventy-five students and an almost completely different faculty from the previous administration. Lee first established a "discreet distance" from the boys of Hargrave Military Academy. Chatham Hall had a six-day academic schedule with Monday set aside for chaperoned girls to walk into Chatham. While Saturday was the Hargrave town day, it was an academic day that included special events for the Chatham Hall girls. In truth, there was little venturing from campus. There were student clubs, but the Girls' Friendly Society and the Cotillion Club continued to reign supreme. An athletic board oversaw a more limited athletic program of class basketball teams.

Chatham Hall was still financially unstable the following year. After graduating twenty-four, one student shy of a third of the school, Chatham Hall continued to struggle for stability. That second year of his heading the school, Lee had to take on eleven "special" students to maintain a student body of seventy-four for the 1929–30 year. The collapse of the stock market in October 1929 and its resulting economic panic should have brought the final blow to Lee's efforts to restore the school; instead, Lee turned the Depression in the school's favor. The South had been economically depressed long before 1929, affecting enrollment during the Powell and Stone administrations. Wages and expenses were already low in 1929, enabling Lee to promote Chatham Hall as a quality education at a bargain price.

Above: Girls gather in the garden in 1929. This more formal garden replaced the one destroyed in the 1906 fire.

Left: Mrs. Lucy Chaplin Lee.

Mrs. Lee was an equally important resource for Chatham Hall at this moment of crisis. As the daughter of Duncan Chaplin, a prominent New York businessman, Lucy Lee had grown up among the social elite of New York City and was a graduate of the prestigious Masters School at Dobbs Ferry. Edmund Lee's family boasted one of the most influential family names in the South. Edmund Lee had often traveled raising funds for the mission in China and enjoyed an entrée to important social and financial circles, where he was both admired and respected.

Together, Edmund and Lucy Lee visited the families of prospective students in the North, advising them that their girls could get the same education for considerably less at Chatham Hall. It worked. The year that followed the stock market crash, Chatham Hall opened with more students than it had enjoyed since 1923. When asked if Chatham Hall was not populated by daughters of the "noveaux riche," Mrs. Lee wryly replied that it was more likely populated by daughters of the "noveaux poor."

Edmund Lee and his wife, Lucy, brought a whole new sense of family to Chatham Hall. With two sons and a daughter, they were parents themselves. That asset, coupled with the experience of having lived within a mission compound since 1912, had accustomed them to the special dynamics occasioned by individuals living closely together. Chatham Hall prospered almost immediately under Dr. Lee. His students adored him, responding to his paternal style of running the school like his own family. He was a firm but fair head of the school who considered each girl his daughter. Mrs. Lee made certain that each girl had a birthday celebration, was invited to tea with her peers and was comforted when sick or distressed. The Lees handled admissions themselves, visiting select cities to interview prospective students. Their admission visit began in Boston, moved to New York and then took in Philadelphia, Pittsburgh, Baltimore and Washington, D.C., before returning to Chatham. There were also side visits to Richmond and Norfolk. The incoming class of new girls had frequently been identified before Christmas with only a few stray vacancies remaining. It was not unusual for a family to camp out in the Bennett Hotel in Chatham at the beginning of the year, hoping that a space would materialize.

Chatham Hall changed rapidly between 1928 and 1931 and then settled down to a successful routine. The 1928–29 session ended the name *Iris* for the yearbook. Its successor, *The Chathamite*, would appear for its first two years as a slender folio edition bound only by a cord. For one of the financially desperate years, the yearbook had to be a section of pictures of the graduating seniors published along with poems and short stories. The

The Chatham Hall campus from the air in 1931.

Girls' Friendly Society was replaced in 1930 by the Service League. It was also the last year that the principal of the school would occupy an apartment in Pruden Hall as Mrs. Willis, Miss Powell and Miss Stone had done. By 1930, the Lees would have to move into the rectory of Emmanuel Episcopal Church to free space for more students.

Chapter 8
Years of Prosperity

Most girls came to Chatham by train, arriving at the Southern Railway depot at the foot of Depot Hill, where they were met by a rickety old school bus driven by Mr. Crute, the superintendent of the farm that supported the Chatham Hall Dairy. They had met a Chatham Hall chaperone, one of the teachers, at Penn Station, New York, or Union Station, Washington, for the final leg of a journey to what must have seemed an island of quiet reason in southern Virginia. There they traded a troubled Depression-era world for the idyllic world of Chatham Hall. The 1930s would turn out to be halcyon years for the school.

By 1933, Chatham Hall was unmistakably the Lees'. By then, the reception well of Pruden Hall had been transformed by painting a lighter ivory over the dark woodwork. Brightly upholstered furniture replaced the gloomy old Mission-style furniture. The small drawing room to the left of the entrance received the same treatment. The short hall between that drawing room and a small private dining room was the main entrance for the main dining room of the school. To the right of the main entrance, the wall between what had been the Lees' living room and the small library was torn down, creating a brighter library that was three times the size of the original.

The Lees had abandoned their school apartment in 1930, moving to the rectory of Emmanuel Episcopal Church on Main Street in Chatham as a means of gaining space on campus for instruction and student rooms. Throughout the 1930s, Dr. Lee would continue to move faculty

Business manager Ed Brush changed the old riding club into a major equestrian program. This photograph is from 1931.

accommodations out of the dormitories, first to gain additional student rooms and also to give the adults more privacy.

There were other noteworthy changes at Chatham Hall after 1930. The old two-hole golf course that had been laid out by the farm manager and later expanded to four holes was given a more professional appearance. The addition of archery and the construction of six tennis courts expanded the athletic offering, but the chief addition to the athletic program was the development of a true riding program. There had been two older farm horses stabled at the barn when Lee arrived in 1928. By 1933, there was a new stable with twenty-one horses, along with a new paddock northwest of the barn. With nearly 90 percent of the students participating, horseback riding had become Chatham Hall's major sport. This program would remain largely trail riding until after World War II.

New girls arrived on the second Tuesday in September. Old girls joined them the following day, and after spending the remainder of the week becoming accustomed to the academic program, both the new girls and the old girls met under the Meadow Oak for the opening picnic. Purple and gold teams were chosen on the first of October. Both semesters were long stretches during those years, with very little travel beyond the campus save for hikes into Chatham or rides across country following an advertised two hundred miles of developed riding trails. The annual Halloween party was a highlight, put on by the team that lost the "Comic Swim Meet" at the beginning of the semester. Juniors traveled annually to Williamsburg, while seniors visited Washington, D.C. Otherwise, girls remained on campus

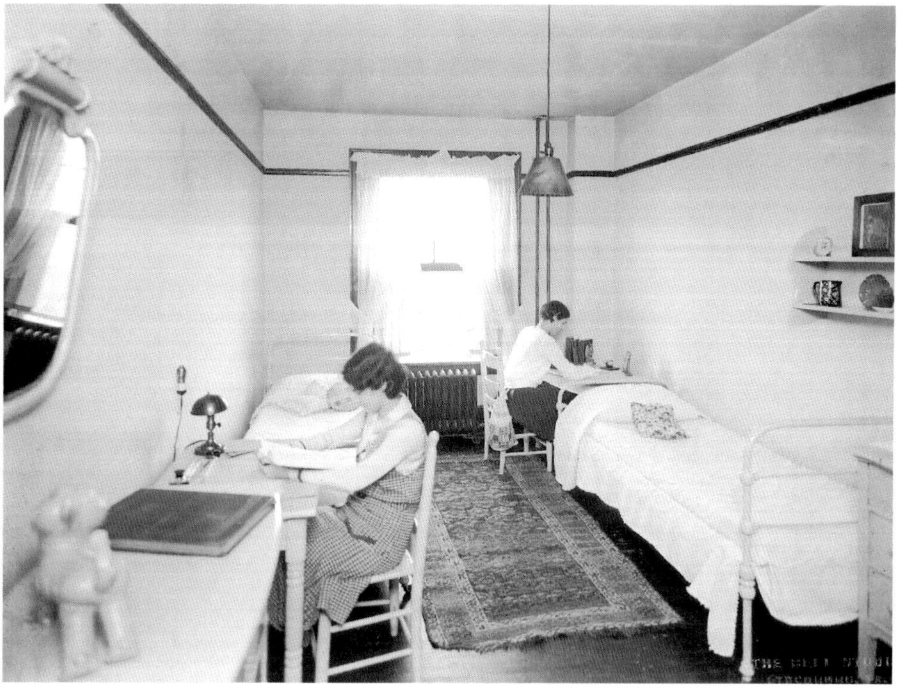

Dorm rooms had not changed much by this 1931 photograph.

until the end of the third week in December, when they left for a two-week Christmas holiday. Thanksgiving was a campus holiday marked by the Sherwood Drama Club performance, a picnic on the meadow and the annual Thanksgiving Dinner.

Final examinations greeted the girls on their return from Christmas holidays, but the faculty cheered the exam gloom with their annual show, ratcheting up spirits for the beginning of the second semester. Although there was a weeklong spring vacation, Easter was celebrated on campus. The now-traditional May Day celebration continued to honor the May Queen and her court. By moving the May Day celebration from the front lawn to the meadow, riders could now participate by competing before the "court" in medieval games on horseback. Dancers and jugglers entertained.

Commencement exercises stretched over the first weekend of June. With exams ending on Saturday, all classes turned their attention to the Purple and Gold Banquet, an athletic event that had replaced the old athletic banquet in 1930. Seniors donned caps and gowns and then trooped to Emmanuel Episcopal Church in Chatham for their baccalaureate service.

The first Chatham Athletic Council. 1931.

Following baccalaureate, relative quiet settled in until the evening vesper service. Officers of the new Service League and other officers were installed at that final vesper service, turning over leadership of the school.

At the closing of vespers, seniors took up their lanterns, followed by the others for the lantern ceremony. Monday was Class Day, with a reception at the Lees' home, followed by the class song contest and the senior play that evening. Tuesday morning was graduation. Once again, seniors donned caps and gowns. Assembling one last time in the Commons Room of Dabney Hall, they received diplomas, marking the end of the school year.

Chatham Hall's academic reputation soared during the 1930s. Writing to the Southern Association of Colleges and Schools in 1937, Lee reported that the Chatham Hall students were "a highly selective group," representing only a fraction of the applicants. One of his favorite anecdotes came from one Chatham Hall father, a neighbor of President Roosevelt's Hyde Park home. He had stopped in to visit the president at Hyde Park before visiting Chatham Hall with his daughter. When the president learned of the application, he remarked, "Oh yes, I've heard of Chatham Hall, of course. But I understand it is ducéd hard to get in there. If they turn you down, I suggest you try getting in at Sweetbriar."

A standard course load during the 1930s included four academic courses, plus religious education that met one to three times a week, depending on the grade level. In addition, each girl took a half-unit course in home economics or art each semester. There were four levels of scholarship with corresponding rewards or strictures. Those in Level A, "Finest Scholarship," had met the dozen tests of citizenship and were, therefore, in complete control of their time, allowed to study where they wished. Those in Level B were permitted to study in their rooms but were not able to leave the room during the two hours of study hall. Those on Level C were obliged to study in the Dabney Study Hall. While these girls did not have special privileges, they did not suffer any social restrictions. Those relegated to Level D studied in the study hall under strict supervision, had time restrictions during the day and were limited in their ability to take part in social programs.

Sadly, Chatham Hall suffered its first and only student death in 1932. During the second week of April, Dr. Wade Hampton Venible noted in his diary that many of the girls had come down with bad colds. Their recovery was a constant worry repeated daily. On April 14, he decided that Sally Sherwood should be taken to the hospital in Danville. Over the next two weeks, Venible noted a "shade" of improvement and even a comment that Sally was "slightly better." Her death on April 29 was simply noted as a call from the hospital at 3:00 a.m. Sally Sherwood is remembered today as the namesake for the Sherwood Drama Club, a memorial bestowed by the girls who had taken part with her in the school's productions.

By 1935, the numbers were more than Pruden and Dabney Halls could accommodate. Writing to alumnae in April 1935, Dr. Lee announced that the school was building a four-story wing at the back of Pruden Hall in order to enlarge the crowded dining room and add some needed dormitory space. Its main level of the annex would house the first new kitchen and equipment since 1907. The former kitchen was demolished, doubling the dining space. A small private dining room across the hall from the small drawing room became Chatham Hall's first student lounge

Equally important was a music room that took up the entire second floor of the new annex. Its main room at the rear of the wing overlooked the old power plant, the swimming pool and a small Victorian-style garden behind the arcade. Two private practice rooms were to either side of the hallway leading to it. Additional dormitory space on the top floor of the wing eased

The new wing behind Pruden removed the kitchens from the main building, enabling the expansion of the dining room.

the crowding problem but at the expense of trimming considerable space from the art studio. Since 1907, that studio had stretched across the end of Pruden Hall. Now the hallway of third-floor Pruden was extended to the end of the building in order to connect with the new wing and to give window light from the north end of Pruden for the hallway. No doubt, girls were happy that by moving the music room, the infirmary could be located on a dormitory floor.

Most exciting was the proposal that the school would build a recreation building at the south end of Dabney Hall. Unlike the new wing, the school would have to raise at least 50 percent of the $15,000 estimated building cost before construction could begin, hopefully in July 1935. Lee's most radical proposal was a campus residence "for Mrs. Lee and myself." The Lee family had abandoned the principal's apartment in Pruden in 1930 to gain space for instruction and had been living in the rectory of the Episcopal Church on Main Street of Chatham, a long walk up Lanier Street from Chatham Hall. Dr. Lee was still both the principal of Chatham Hall and the rector of Emmanuel Episcopal Church. Chatham Hall students had been attending Emmanuel since its opening as CEI in 1894. They had always been received as honored guests at the rectory, but it was enough of a daunting walk that students seldom made the trip, aside from traveling to their usual Sunday service. Now Dr. Lee wanted a house that would be "a center in the life of the students, the faculty,

Willis Recreation Building.

visiting alumnae and parents," which he noted, for the present structure, was "quite impossible."

Construction of a new recreation building began during the summer of 1935. Up until that point, the commons room of Dabney Hall had served as auditorium, gymnasium, dance floor and study hall. Even with the curtaining of its stage a few years earlier, the room was hardly adequate for a proper drama program, and moving desks around to accommodate varied functions was hardly practical. The new building was to be named Willis Hall, honoring Elizabeth May Willis as a token of the school's "great admiration and affection." Its auditorium would be flat, rather than raked, so that it could be used for dances and athletic events as well as plays and other performances, but its stage would have a permanent cyclorama and dressing rooms on the lower level that could be reached by a spiral staircase at the rear of the stage. Space was also given over for set construction and storage. At the back of the auditorium, a light booth housed a sound motion picture projector, an addition that would enable Chatham Hall to expand both entertainment and instruction.

One of the most important features of Willis Hall was the "Pine Room" on the lower level, directly under the stage. This was, as Lee described it, a "lovely pine paneled room" furnished in early American style that opened onto a terrace where students lounged in warmer weather. A large open fireplace dominated this student lounge, enhanced by a hand-wrought firescreen and irons, specially forged iron equipment given by the class of 1935. The Pine Room was a more informal successor to the "Tea Room" that had been opened in a Dabney basement room in 1924 by Mrs. Crute, wife of the farm manager. At that time, it was a small restaurant where girls would order a sandwich and a drink from a waitress just as they would in a "real" restaurant. First intended as a means of teaching manners and social graces, the original Tea Room had quickly become a favorite refuge. Now the Willis Hall Pine Room would be a place where students could relax and enjoy snacks or a sandwich. In later years, it would again assume the name "Tea Room," passing through frequent metamorphoses as students changed, but it has always remained a popular retreat.

Construction on this new recreation building had begun at the same time that a measles epidemic swept through the school, forcing all of the "well" girls to live in Dabney Hall while Pruden Hall was turned into a hospital ward for the thirty-five who had been infected. Shortly after graduation ceremonies in 1936, just before faculty members departed for the summer, Dr. and Mrs. Lee hosted a "Castle in Spain" picnic in a grove of trees across from the new Willis Hall that was to be the site for the new residence.

The building of a campus residence for the head of the school was to be the third significant event of 1936 that would shake off Chatham Hall's lingering image as a provincial school. Mrs. Lee had revived the alumnae association in 1933 by inviting alumnae for the first-annual luncheon meeting in New York the following year. By 1936, the annual New York luncheon had become a tradition. That year, the construction of the new recreation building drew Mrs. Willis, as well as her guest and former student, Georgia O'Keeffe, to the Hotel Roosevelt. Later that spring, Mrs. Willis finally returned to Chatham for the dedication of the building that was to honor her eighteen years as head of the school.

Now on a warm June day, faculty gathered where contractors had taped out the shape of a new residence for the head of the school. Named the "Rectory," as its resident was both the rector of Emmanuel Church and principal of Chatham Hall, the home would be a defining element in the tone set by Dr. and Mrs. Lee. Their house in Anking,

The Rectory.

China, had been a social center for the American Church Mission. They frequently entertained clergy and others connected to mission work. Chinese guests were also welcomed as Dr. and Mrs. Lee worked to span the two cultures. Clearly, Dr. Lee viewed the Rectory at Chatham Hall in the same manner. As soon as the family occupied it during the 1936 Christmas holiday, the Rectory became the center of campus life, as Dr. and Mrs. Lee had promised. By the time the Rectory opened, the site had been graced by a metal sign depicting the four grade levels of Chatham Hall. At the far left is a senior, dressed in academic regalia. She carries her diploma in her right hand and leads the junior with her left. The junior carries a lantern in her left hand, symbolizing her acceptance of leadership. By tradition, juniors never touch the lantern until it is given by a senior the night before graduation. The sophomore wears a daisy chain that looks a little like a boa draped over her shoulders. By tradition

Jean Ballin Crump (CEI 1937) designed the Rectory sign. It continues to remind students of their progress from freshmen to seniors. *Photo by Catherine M. LaDuke.*

at that time, sophomores carried a daisy chain to honor the graduating seniors. The freshman, depicted as a young girl, carries the daisy she has picked to help build the daisy chain. Within a short time, the sign, designed by Jean Ballin Crump (class of 1937), became one of Chatham Hall's icons.

Chapter 9

The Vision for St. Mary's

Naming the principal's residence the Rectory had obvious religious connotations. Girls had been attending receptions at the Emmanuel Episcopal Church rectory from the time Dr. and Mrs. Lee had made it their residence. Chatham Hall had been founded on the principal of providing an education grounded in the Christian faith, but there was not a permanent chapel on the campus until 1939. From the outset, CEI girls had gathered for morning prayer daily except Sundays in the parlor of the old Gilmer home, the site of the first school. Sundays, each girl dressed in her required blue church dress, donned her "Institute Cap" and marched down the hill, up College Avenue, and turned right onto Main Street carrying her Bible and her prayer book to Emmanuel Episcopal Church. Teachers walked along with them, no doubt discouraging the interest of local boys.

When CEI moved into Pruden Hall in 1907, following the disastrous fire of 1906, that service of morning prayer was held in the new reception hall, an area now called the "Well." After Dabney Hall opened in 1912, the morning-prayer service moved to a new auditorium called the "Commons." That daily service remained in the same area even after it had been converted into a study hall. Sunday services remained at Emmanuel Church on Main Street.

When Dr. Edmund Jennings Lee arrived in 1928, he had come as both the rector of Emmanuel Episcopal Church in Chatham and the principal of Chatham Hall. Dr. Lee always wanted to have a more permanent chapel on campus along with the church on Main Street in Chatham. His first attempt was an outdoor "woodland chapel" located in a wooded area that is now the upper hockey field. His first indoor chapel on campus was a converted chemistry classroom and lab at the north end of the lower level of Dabney Hall under the study hall. Its heavy dark blue curtains and brass sconces gave it the feel of a chapel, but it was far too small to comfortably accommodate the entire school.

Everything changed in 1937. After forty-three years, Chatham Hall girls would no longer walk to services in Chatham. Dr. Lee announced in January 1937 that a campus chapel had become an "immediate necessity." Ties between the school and the church in town had, as he said, "been severed." Dr. Lee had decided to resign as rector of Emmanuel Episcopal Church. It was difficult enough being the head of Chatham Hall. Having charge of the church and the school at the same time was too great a burden. It is also important to note that the governance of the school had changed. Chatham Hall had been founded as a parish school and had been governed by a local board of trustees composed of local clergy. By the mid-1930s, the board of trustees had changed to a group of men and women from different parts of the country, representing different callings.

Lynchburg architect Trueheart Poston, who had already designed the new recreational building, the Faculty Cottage, the Faculty Club and the Rectory, proposed a chapel design that returned to the pillared, Neoclassical architecture of Pruden and Dabney. Seating 250 at an estimated cost of $25,000, this new building would be, in Dr. Lee's words, "gothic in feeling." From the very beginning, the proposed new chapel was named Tucker Memorial Chapel honoring Bishop Beverley Dandridge Tucker, the bishop of southern Virginia. It had been Bishop Tucker who had attempted to heal the breach between Elizabeth May Willis and Orlando Pruden that marked the beginning of the decline that had continued through the 1920s. It was he who had called Edmund Lee to Chatham in 1928 to help save Chatham Hall from bankruptcy.

Even as an "immediate" necessity, the school could not afford the chapel. The cost was estimated at $25,000, but the school had overextended its building fund by constructing four new buildings in rapid succession since 1935. There was, however, no greater urgency for Dr. Lee. He saw this chapel not only as a place of worship but also as a link between the present and the past of the school. As such, it would also be a memorial to those "who have passed beyond" provided by "those living who love and wish to commemorate them." Donations to the chapel fund came in slowly

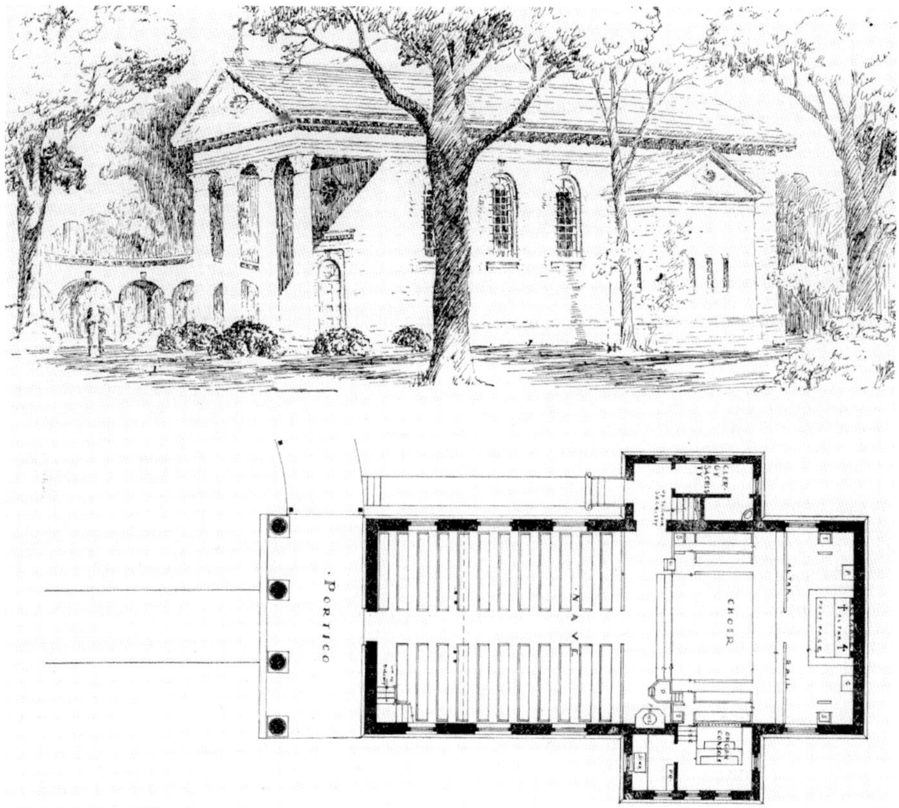

The 1938 proposed chapel.

between Lee's first announcement and the next alumnae newsletter, but the $9,000 collected by January 1938 swelled to $18,900 by June, and Lee had become "very enthusiastic about the part our old students and their families are playing in the construction." That June 1938 alumnae newsletter also published a revised design for a new proposed façade, one more in keeping with the colonial brick of other buildings. Even with the anticipated cost growing to $30,000, enthusiasm seemed to be growing. The class of 1938 had already pledged a rose window that would depict the annunciation to St. Mary. Four of the twelve windows proposed for the sanctuary had also been donated.

Unfortunately, chapel euphoria was short-lived. When contractors reviewed the plans for Tucker Memorial Chapel, they estimated actual construction would cost $60,000, not $30,000. Even trimming $5,000 in expenses that could be delayed, the chapel building fund was woefully short. After recovering from the initial shock, Lee wrote to other Episcopal schools to find out what their chapels had cost, finding some "comfort" in learning that prices had ranged from $100,000 to $1 million. After all, he wrote, "for a school that lays as much emphasis on beauty and on religion as we do, a $60,000 chapel was perhaps not excessive."

Even if the estimate was not excessive, the chapel fund was still short over $40,000, but Dr. Lee had promised a chapel, one that would be built through gifts, so he turned to the banks for temporary help and, with trustee approval, borrowed $15,000, to be paid over the next three years, so that construction could begin before the girls returned for the 1938–39 session. He barely made it in time. The first shovel of dirt was turned on September 20, a mere three days ahead of the girls. Lee himself wrote to the alumnae in the fall 1938 *Chat* regarding his vision for the new chapel:

> *The chapel when it is complete will represent our students, past and present, and their families, with the trustees, the faculty, and the friends of the school. It will represent the affection and loyalty of every one to the school and devotion to the ideals for which it stands. It will represent giving, often to the point of sacrifice, and many of these gifts will be memorials. In this way it will bind all the past of the school to the present, and will relate our world to the eternal world, which is just what a chapel should do.*

It was going to be a long struggle to "complete" this chapel. Lee tirelessly sought additional funds throughout the year, even scrounging an old Wurlitzer organ that had stood idle in a Danville movie theater since the invention of sound motion pictures. Not the organ desired, but good enough to serve temporarily.

When students, faculty and guests crowded in front of the new construction on June 2, 1939, their chapel was a rough building that taxed the imagination. Workmen had been laboring late into the night for the previous two weeks to complete the "necessary" work. Burlap covered raw block and brick where there should have been oak paneling. Footsteps resonated on a bare concrete floor, and the choir sat on temporary chairs as no one had yet donated the woodwork for the front of the chapel. The congregation had to depend on imagination to picture a finished chapel as they sang "For All the Saints Who from Their Labors Rest." Construction costs of $43,000 had exhausted the chapel building fund. There was much to be done.

That summer of 1939, Dr. Lee still needed to raise $16,000, $6,750 of which was immediately necessary to make the chapel usable for the coming school year. However, there were other building projects that were almost as important. By building faculty residences, the dormitory rooms and apartments that had been occupied by teachers could be turned into student

Dr. Lee leads a chapel service in this undated photograph.

rooms. This would be a priority, as tuition generated the operating budget money for many years to come. Some teachers had lived in Chatham in a rented home referred to as the "Teachery." Now a new faculty house for four single teachers called the Faculty Cottage was being built down the hill from Dabney Hall.

Beside the Faculty Cottage, Lee added the Faculty Club at the bottom of the garden. Faculty who lived in dorms had no place to receive guests other than the public drawing room. Faculty social gatherings were impossible on campus. The Faculty Club was the attempt to do something specifically for the faculty. To the south of the Faculty Cottage, Lee was also constructing a handsome "Deanery" for Dean Virginia Holt. Two more buildings would be added within the next two years: a cottage across from the chapel that would gain the name the "Mite Box" and a larger home in a grove of trees near the Rectory named for Pansy Andrus, the music teacher.

Three controversies regarding the chapel had to be settled. The name "Tucker Memorial Chapel" was dropped in favor of "St. Mary's Chapel," although the building would remain a memorial to Beverly Dandridge Tucker. The pew versus chair debate divided the school until Dr. Lee reported to the alumnae in January 1941 that the "intelligent minority" that had always stood for chairs was "triumphantly vindicated." The new chairs were, as Lee described them, "beautiful and comfortable…silent and churchly." A final controversy arose over the death of a bird, a red-headed woodpecker killed when workers were trying to get it out of the chapel for the opening service. Girls were upset that one of God's creatures had been sacrificed to clear the chapel for God's service of worship, something that struck them as somewhat sacrilegious. The furor settled when Dr. Lee promised to memorialize the bird in one of the nave windows. This is the St. Francis Window, the first to the right facing the altar. The hands of the figure of St. Francis point to a blue bird and to a woodpecker.

Again, Lee turned to the alumnae asking for as little as $0.80 for one of the foot-square stone tiles or as much as $600 for a stained-glass window. Lee was determined that the chapel was to be built entirely from donations, but it would need 17,500 of the stone tiles, eleven more windows, 220 feet of oak paneling at $10 per foot and fifteen light fixtures at $50 per fixture.

Chapter 10
War Years

Chatham Episcopal Institute had not been deeply affected by World War I. Once, the girls assembled in front of Pittsylvania County's courthouse in Chatham to listen to a patriotic speech by Dr. Pruden when Richard Willis returned from the front with the French Croix de Guerre. As the son of the head of the school who had been a student at CEI until the tenth grade, Richard Willis was CEI's contribution to the war. There were other young men who came through in uniform—brothers, friends and a few fathers—but there was no other personal connection for the girls. Even trooping en masse into Chatham singing patriotic songs to celebrate the armistice was only temporary.

World War II was different. From its outset, the war became a personal battle for many girls. Beyond the homefront activities like preparing bandages and raising money for relief programs, Chatham Hall girls would harbor and help heal several girls who found refuge from war in Virginia. Too frequently, they would share grief. As alumnae, they would go to war, some as nurses, some as officers in women's units of the army and navy and some ferrying unarmed aircraft to England, returning just to repeat that perilous journey again and again. No brass bands, no medals—just determined service.

The war came early for Chatham Hall, long before Pearl Harbor. Dr. Lee had been a missionary in China for twenty-five years. He and his wife had close connections to Americans and Chinese. The invasion of China by the Empire of Japan was especially distressing for him, particularly the brutal bombing of Shanghai. Chatham Hall's first notion of war came when Dr. Lee introduced a girl who had come to Chatham Hall after escaping the invasion of Shanghai. Through her, Chatham Hall girls learned that the beauty of moonlight on the front campus was the kind of light favored by enemy pilots because they could see targets below. Death came by moonlight in this new twisted world.

Even with such personal awareness of suffering, Chatham Hall remained a place of calm, an island refuge from the news that came out of Munich, the Sudetenland, Poland and France. Of course, the war came home on December 7, 1941. Local officials quickly devised civil defense plans that included Chatham Hall as an evacuation first-aid station in the event of attack. All girls learned first-aid procedures. Painters changed the white dome of Pruden Hall to a dull gray to match the slate roofs and also painted over the Well skylight to eliminate the ability of enemy bombers to detect Pruden Hall. Girls practiced air raid evacuation and learned how to function during blackouts with student wardens. Many girls spent time in the Red Cross Room preparing dressings, twenty-seven thousand each semester. Eventually, the congestion of troop movements on the Southern Railway forced the school to lengthen Christmas vacation and eliminate spring vacation. Students were on campus from September to mid-December and from mid-January until the first week of June. After 1941, there was no longer an annual May Day festival, and few guests were able to attend graduation exercises.

The most significant change in the school was curricular. Dr. Lee felt strongly that the war was, in part, the result of isolationism. A new generation

The Red Cross Room.

had to be "international to the heart's core, recognizing the brotherhood of humanity and the solidarity of the world." For Lee, that solidarity would translate into first enabling students to have a greater consciousness of their duties as citizens. Senior English classes focused on the development of American democracy. American history classes conducted current affairs

A 1940s dorm room.

programs for the school. It was Dr. Lee's opinion that America must either improve democracy or lose it. The war would show which way it was to be. An enlightened, responsible citizenry was essential. To that end, Chatham Hall formed a Citizenship League made up of seniors, all members of the faculty and alumnae who lived in the Chatham area. This league brought speakers to the campus. Its members addressed current events, as well as the problems of democracy, and eventually focused on the problems that would arise for a postwar world.

There was never a serious shortage of food during the war, especially as the school had its own farm, even though there was a shortage of labor for farming and harvesting. Gasoline and tires were a different matter. Ed Brush, the business manager, purchased an old army wagon and two mules for carrying mail and delivering milk from the school's dairy. Soon "Giggles" and "Goggles" became a regular feature seen routinely by the girls. Sadly, sometimes the news of a battle death came while letters were still arriving from the front. A girl would disappear into the Rectory to stay with Dr. and Mrs. Lee for a few days, or a girl might be seen taking a long walk with Miss Holt, deep in troubled conversation, but it was the family on dorm that had learned best how to support those who had lost someone.

The July 1943 *Chat* began publishing lists of alumnae engaged in war service, first reporting six navy Women Accepted for Voluntary Emergency Service (WAVES), twelve army Women's Army Corps (WACS) and eight others. Lee spoke of "the stern demands of these days" and praised alumnae for their "intelligence, adaptability and the ability to work hard." Lee also felt that women would have to shoulder the enormous responsibility of restoring civilization following the war. Most men's schools had shelved history, social science and literature courses for the duration of the war. Women would have to hold up the "intellectual front in order to train "the navigators of the world of tomorrow." The whole sense of strength and effort even found its way into a new song for graduation in 1943. Instead of the "Alma Mater," the class of 1943 sang a new song with words written by Emily Allen and music by Elizabeth Sinclair. "Sunlit Pillars" began with the "joyous laughter" of day-to-day life in a school where teams contend and friendships strengthen, but its second stanza changes the focus to "straining" and "striving," "strength of soul" and "dauntless spirit." These were qualities students would need even more before the end of the war.

Chapter 11

Looking Forward

Like other schools and colleges, Chatham Hall had started planning for the postwar period as early as 1944, but finishing the chapel was no longer the priority. Chatham Hall needed to renovate old structures and modernize just about everything. A new classroom building was planned for the area directly behind Willis Hall, now Lee Library. Planned as an architectural match to the other buildings on campus, the proposed building was to cost what was considered a staggering $90,000. Unfortunately, the estimate did not account for a stupefying postwar inflation. With the lifting of wartime price controls, construction costs doubled and then doubled again. By the time Chatham Hall had raised the money, $90,000 would never build such a magnificent classroom building.

As intended, St. Mary's Chapel linked the present to the past. The war brought St. Mary's chapel one of its most beautiful memorial legacies. Seven girls had lost brothers during the war, all in the later years during bitter fighting in both Europe and the Pacific. Wartime St. Mary's Chapel had been a place of prayer and comfort. Here girls reached out for healing, finding it in their faith and in the girls who prayed with them. That healing is the source of the bas-relief of the Madonna and child over the front door of St. Mary's chapel. Sculptor John Angel's bas-relief not only memorializes those seven brothers, but it also remains a continual reminder of the comforting embrace of 150 sisters, a whole community of love.

Chatham Hall quietly celebrated its fiftieth anniversary in 1944. By January 1945, Lee would observe that the "joyfulness" of Chatham Hall had been "tempered by the background of sadness." With hundreds in service and the recent loss of seven brothers, the whole school shared "anxiety and sorrow." Part of this pain came through letters from alumnae who poured out their grief to Dr. Lee. "Our hearts go out to them," he wrote in the *Chat*, "and there is deep satisfaction in sharing their grief." As the numbers involved in the war effort grew, Lee could not help observing, "We must seek to build a new world worthy of this great sacrifice." To this he added a confirmation: "It can be done."

The final school year of the war began with a "siege" of rain that wrought its own devastation. Rain started during the opening faculty dinner, becoming such a heavy downpour that teachers were drenched by the time they reached the safety of their homes. Chatham Hall only suffered with the flooding of Dabney Hall and the Rectory basements, but the old Moses Mill, one of the sites of Chatham Hall's annual Easter picnic, washed off its foundation. By the time it finally came to rest against the railway bridge at the south end of Chatham, service on the entire railway system south of Washington had been suspended. Girls on their way to Chatham were trapped in Washington's Union Station when the service was cut, so chaperones traded in tickets to Chatham for ones that took the whole group first to Richmond and then to Greensboro, North Carolina, via Raleigh. Into their second day of travel, the girls finally boarded buses in Greensboro for the last leg of the journey. Unfortunately, there was little comfort when they arrived in Chatham. With the town's water supply having been contaminated during the flood, there was no water for bathing, nor would there be until the second week of school. Old wells behind Pruden Hall yielded enough water for cooking and drinking, but nothing was left for laundry or bathing. Perhaps the greatest disaster was the loss of mail delivery when the trains stopped running.

Such discomforts had become a part of the homefront during the war, largely because materials and labor were directed toward armaments. When the boilers for the heating plant went out in mid-winter 1944, there was no way to immediately replace them. Girls bundled up in whatever woolens they had. Classes were moved to the few homes on campus that had heat, but everywhere else was cold. A fire was kept going in the fireplace of the small drawing room until it burned through its chimney and into the dining room directly behind it. Fortunately, lunch was just being served; the fire was immediately detected, and a second major fire in the school's history was averted. It was a full week before the boilers could be repaired.

By graduation in 1945, the war in Europe was over. Even with the war in the Pacific still going, a group of fathers urged Dr. Lee to begin planning for the postwar future of Chatham Hall. That April, Dr. Lee had received a letter from a father expressing his opinion that it was a "highly favorable" time to launch a development campaign. Within a week of Lee's having received the letter, the board of trustees endorsed a capital campaign for the construction of a new classroom building. Their initial plan was to send letters to the seven hundred families that then made up the "Chatham Hall Family." A development committee then met in New York to launch the campaign, as time "was of the essence." The goal was $150,000, $90,000 of which was dedicated to a new classroom building. The rest of the money would be used to upgrade the school's existing infrastructure.

The July 1945 *Chat* was full of plans for a total overhaul of the school's facilities. Addressing alumnae directly, Lee noted that the "greatness of a school is in its personnel, its spirit and traditions," but he also conceded that equipment was nearly as important. Chatham Hall needed to refurbish classrooms and remove the ones located in the basement of Dabney Hall. A new classroom building would enable the school to move the library out of Pruden Hall into the area of Dabney Hall that had been vacated. That would in turn enable the school to turn the old Pruden Hall library into a student lounge. The dining room was overcrowded; there were too few tennis courts and no real indoor athletic facility. Girls needed an area where they could change for riding. One more athletic field should be developed, preferably in an area behind the Faculty Cottage, the Faculty Club and the Deanery.

An architect's rendering of the proposed academic building appeared on the first page of the February 1946 *Chat*. Designed to hold fourteen classrooms, the building would be located directly behind Willis Hall, leaving a connecting space that would serve as an outdoor terrace for the Pine Room. Sadly, however, that issue also includes a lament that the campaign was not progressing as rapidly as had been thought. Only a little over half the goal, $76,000, had been contributed. Lee huffed that "many boy's schools, not a whit more prominent or popular, are raising successfully much larger funds."

The notion that donations were going to support boys rather than girls was a new public topic for Dr. Lee. Earlier, when questioned why Chatham Hall did not teach home economics to prepare girls for domestic life, Lee responded, "It does not seem to us…that a course in cooking is the wisest use of time during these precious years in which we have our students." The issue was one of educational philosophy that set Chatham Hall apart from other girl's boarding schools. "The education of women," Lee mused, "is still

The old stables.

comparatively new. Many families still do not take seriously the education of daughters and think that a little superficial polish of the kind given by some 'finishing schools' is all that is needed. We at Chatham Hall hold exactly the contrary opinion." Clearly, Lee was frustrated with the tepid response, so much so that after asking alumnae to contact their families to take up the matter of a donation "persuasively and convincingly," he referred to the work he and his wife had done since 1938 to establish Chatham Hall as a nationally prominent school. He wanted to retire, but he did not want his term to be little more than an "episode" after which the school would "slip into mediocrity."

Normalcy began to return with the 1945 graduation exercises. Once again, there was the song contest and Purple and Gold banquet on Saturday, the lantern ceremony following the final vesper service on Sunday and the full range of Class Day activities on Monday with a family picnic in the meadow, the dedication of the yearbook and tea at the Rectory with the Lees. There was even room for two new traditions. The first had the outgoing student council members announce their successors on the steps of Pruden Hall rather than in the chapel during vespers. Now there was metal for a new council pin given by the outgoing council member to a successor. The second new tradition was a senior banquet held in the Pine Room of Willis Hall to lead off the days of graduation festivities. By fall, things were almost as they had been before the war. Students returned to Williamsburg and Washington for class trips; boys, many still in uniform, were again invited for a formal dance.

After being delayed by the war, Dr. Lee returned to the question of finishing the chapel, not that the chapel was ever far from his mind, even during the war. In 1944, knowing that Americans had few consumer goods on which to spend high wartime wages, he challenged alumnae chapters in Boston, Chicago, Detroit, Houston, New York, Philadelphia and Pittsburgh to be responsible for the oak woodwork in the chapel. The "Girls of the Seven Cities" represented the largest contingents of Chatham Hall girls. Happily, there were seven bays in the chapel now covered by burlap, one each for the seven alumnae groups. The New York chapter had already raised enough to pay for one of the seven bays. Ever the practical man, Lee offered to accept donations in the form of war stamps or war bonds, a gesture that would be both patriotic and philanthropic. By January 1948, he was able to report that the chapel was nearly complete; all that remained was to build its tower and install the chimes.

For twenty years, students and faculty had chuckled over little stories of Dr. Lee's absent-mindedness. There were stories in Chatham about his having forgotten parking his car in town and finding out only after he had walked back to campus. Some suggested that he may have cultivated the "absent-minded professor" image just as students learned to "read" the fluttering of his eyebrows to discern his mood. One instance of absent-mindedness was true. Dr. Lee handled admissions work for the school, traveling to selected cities, where he would interview prospective students. Interviews in New York City were held in the Biltmore Hotel, near Grand Central Station. One day, while standing in the lobby, Lee spied a familiar woman exiting an elevator. Certain she was a Chatham Hall alumna whose name he had simply forgotten, Lee strode over and greeted her saying "Pardon me, are you one of my old girls?" "No," was the reply, "I'm Eleanor Roosevelt."

The prospect of mistaking Eleanor Roosevelt apparently did not ruffle Dr. Lee. After apologizing for his mistake, he first described Chatham Hall, explained that he was doing admissions interviews and ended with an invitation to visit Chatham. Mrs. Roosevelt was charmed and later accepted.

On Valentines Day 1948, Mrs. Lee met Mrs. Roosevelt at Sweetbriar College and drove her to Chatham. Four days before her arrival, the area

Girls at the old bus.

had been paralyzed by six inches of snow and it was still cold, but Willis Hall was packed with people from the town as well as Chatham Hall students and faculty. After Dr. Lee introduced her as a "true American who had become a great world citizen," Mrs. Roosevelt spoke to the girls about her experience as chairman of the Commission on Human Rights and her commission's difficulty in framing a declaration of human rights that would be satisfactory to a diversity of nationalities.

Each student, Mrs. Roosevelt said, had a duty to learn as much as possible about the fledgling United Nations, declaring that nations must make the "machinery of the United Nations work for the establishment of world peace." She warned that the United States was not assured safety, even with the secret of the atomic bomb, reminding her audience of the incomparable destruction in Europe wrought with conventional weapons. After her speech and dinner at the Rectory, Mrs. Roosevelt boarded the train to continue a lecture tour.

By 1948, most Chatham Hall alumnae had known only one head of school. Along with other sweeping changes following the war, it was now time for Chatham Hall to enter into a new era. Alumnae had first learned of the Lees' intent to retire when they heard it from Dr. Lee himself at the annual New York luncheon held at the Hotel Beekman on February 15, 1947. Edmund and Lucy Lee had been a successful team. He had guided the school through the difficult years when the quagmire of debt threatened to suck it under and then had turned the Depression to the school's advantage to establish a boarding school with a national reputation for high academic standards and finally had been its pilot through the stormy war years. Mrs. Lee had instituted a Service League that had inculcated the ideal of Christ-like service. Both Edmund and Lucy Lee considered Christ-like service to be the guiding principle of Chatham Hall.

A revived alumnae association was Lucy Lee's creation, as was its newsletter, the *Chat*. More than other traditions, girls had become accustomed to the Monday birthday parties in the Rectory for those whose birthday fell during that week. These girls had also been whisked away from the infirmary when ill to recuperate with the Lee family, just as if they had gone home.

Now there was some anxiety about the future, especially as two traditions, one for the girls and one for alumnae, seemed in peril. The first was the society of "Biabues," a loosely defined group Lee concocted sometime in the late 1930s, although he could never remember exactly when. The Biabues was an organization without organization, rules, officers or official meetings. Biabues had to be good citizens, very friendly and have a "whimsical" personality. There was no election. New members were "discovered" when Lee gathered the old Biabues together after lunch to draw up a list of honorees. New Biabues were "taken in" at the following lunch, when old Biabues tapped them out. It was just simple fun.

The other tradition was the writing of annual birthday cards to all alumnae, a practice Lee adopted in 1938 from Dr. Endicott Peabody, the head of Groton School. In writing each, Lee tried to recall the personality of the girl and wished her God's blessing for "finest development and deepest happiness." If the alumna was married, he also asked for blessings for her husband and children. These blessings included "clearer apprehension of truth, deeper faith in reality, wisdom, power and love of the Eternal Father, conformity to His will, dedication to his service."

While the board of trustees searched for a suitable replacement, it voted to name the new academic building "Lee Hall," but even naming the building for such a popular head of school failed to inspire giving. The fund had reached only $115,000 by the spring of 1948, almost three years after it had been launched. Part of the money raised had already gone into tearing out the dietician's office in order to enlarge the dining room and toward the construction of new tennis courts. Lee let his frustration show when he announced his retirement at the meeting of the New York Alumnae Association. Speaking of his then eighteen years as head of Chatham

Tea with Mrs. Lee became a popular tradition.

Hall, Lee noted that there had been a "happy combination of policies and personalities" that had made Chatham Hall what he called a "nation-wide school." Now he hoped that "these wonderful years shall not be a mere episode in the life of the school."

Graduation came for the class of 1949. The chapel tower was under construction. The Pittsburgh Alumnae Chapter presented a portrait of William Pitt, earl of Chatham, the namesake for the town of Chatham and Pittsylvania County. As the Pitt family coat of arms figures prominently in the Chatham Hall coat of arms, the portrait was an appropriate addition for the entrance hall. A portrait of Lee would come later, as would a building named in his honor. As the building fund neared its original goal, inflation had pushed the estimated cost of constructing the new academic structure out of the school's reach. It would never be built.

Despite the disappointment over the new classroom building, St. Mary's Chapel's tower and steeple were now in place. Mrs. Arthur Kelly Evans still wanted the campus to have chimes for the chapel, so she had given money for a chapel tower in lieu of a contribution to the classroom building. The completed chapel tower fulfilled Dr. Lee's vision. Its chimes finally rang—just as Dr. Lee retired.

Chapter 12

The First "Rector"

By the end of the war, the community of Chatham Hall knew that it was time to find a successor for Dr. Lee. He had been its leader since 1928, essentially molding the school to fit his vision after having saved it from what seemed financial disaster in 1928. Lee was legendary, certainly a difficult person to replace. Between 1928 and the end of the war, he had so secured the school's academic reputation that the families of girls on the waiting list frequently brought their daughters to stay at a local hotel in the hope that a place at Chatham Hall would magically appear. Almost as frequently, the chance to enroll never materialized. Lee had been instrumental in adding a wing to Pruden Hall and in constructing the Willis Hall auditorium and recreation center. Student life had been drastically revised, with greater involvement in student government and community service. Religious life was greatly altered by the construction of St. Mary's Chapel. In many respects, Chatham Hall *was* Edmund Lee. With his wife, Lucy Chaplin Lee, the two had been the first husband-and-wife duo to affect the lives of students as a team since the two years under William Clarkson Marshall between 1900 and 1902. By 1948, Chatham Hall had known no other leadership than the Lees' for twenty years, almost half of the school's history. The majority of the alumnae had known only the Lees. Essentially, Chatham Hall was their school.

The prospect of Chatham Hall under anyone other than the Lees was unsettling. Dr. Lee, himself, had written to his girls, the alumnae, as early as 1947 that he and Lucy were planning to retire, but there was a hint of reluctance in his announcement. Too much work had gone into establishing Chatham Hall as a nationally prominent boarding school. Lee did not want that national prominence to slip into mediocrity. The right person to lead would continue to strengthen the school. In an extraordinary demonstration of confidence in Lee's sense of what was right for Chatham Hall, the board of trustees allowed him to conduct the search for his own replacement, although they reserved the final appointment for themselves. Preferably, the new head of the school would be an Episcopal clergyman to carry on the relationship between church and school. It was also important that new head of the school and his spouse would be a team in much the same manner as Edmund and Lucy Lee.

The opportunity came through a Chatham Hall parent. Alice Murray's daughters had attended the Tuxedo Park Country Day School in Tuxedo Park, New York, before entering Chatham Hall. Its young headmaster had taken over a financially troubled school at the end of World War II and had wrought wonders. Now she suggested to Lee that the young man might be the right choice for Chatham Hall. Edmund Lee wrote to William Woolsey Yardley on February 24, 1948, telling him of Mrs. Murray's suggestion that they meet. He and Lucy would be in New York interviewing admission candidates at the Biltmore Hotel, so they had an opportunity to meet William and Helen Yardley over an extended lunch. While Lee was impressed enough at that initial encounter to invite the Yardleys to Chatham the following April, there was an immediate problem in that William Yardley was not a clergyman. The visit to Chatham was successful, but even with an announced willingness to enter the ministry, not currently being a clergyman seemed to squash any hope that William Yardley would succeed Edmund Lee. It was not until the early summer of 1948 that the trustees agreed to set aside their concern regarding Yardley's lack of ordination and at least consider his candidacy. It was evident that the Yardleys were the kind of husband-and-wife team that Edmund Lee felt would be best for Chatham Hall.

There is a tone of regret in Edmund Lee's communications just prior to his retirement. The grand plans that had been so hopefully launched at the end of Word War II were not progressing as had been expected. Support for the major capital campaign limped on. While there were new athletic fields and the chapel tower was finally under construction, the grand academic building that was to be named in Lee's honor was out of the range of the money that was being raised. With a hopeful note that support for Chatham Hall would not vanish with his retirement, Edmund Lee wrote to alumnae,

Dr. William Woolsey Yardley.

students and parents in February 1949, asking them to maintain their "loyalty and devotion to Chatham Hall" even without the Lees. The sentiment was echoed in a photograph taken of the Lees and the Yardleys on the porch of the Rectory, effectively suggesting that the school would endure even if there was a changing of the guard. As Edmund and Lucy Lee drove down the hill on their way to their third-floor flat in Washington, D.C., the chapel bells rang for the first time. The Yardleys, with their two children, moved temporarily into the old Brush House residence behind Dabney Hall while the Rectory was repainted.

Concerns that a new administration would change Chatham Hall quieted during William Yardley's first year as head of the school. There was a new title for the position. Edmund Lee had been principal of the school and

The Lees and the Yardleys pose together in front of the Rectory to mark a significant transition for Chatham Hall.

rector of the St. Mary's Chapel. Now the title of rector would stand for both positions. There was even a brief note in the spring 1950 issue of the *Chat* announcing with some relief that "the new rector has not changed the school." There was the usual February school dance with young men arriving from Williams and Harvard. That year, Willis Hall was decorated as a huge aviary, its walls draped in green gossamer fabric. Huge birds were placed against the walls and suspended from the ceiling. The Sherwood Drama Club presented *Candida* and *The Devil and Daniel Webster*.

There was a new school bus for longer trips, but such outings were still relatively few, so girls continued to walk into Chatham on Mondays. There was a momentary rabies scare that seized the attention of the campus. Girls had mistaken a small, black dog that had wandered on campus for the Yardley's dog, Dickie. Even when it was clearly not the Rectory dog, girls forbore complaining when they were nipped and even hid the infected dog in the dorm for several nights until it mysteriously died. Unfortunately, the stray was buried before being tested for rabies, so as a precaution, thirty-two students and Dean Holt had to suffer through the Pasteur treatment's painful series of shots. Shared experience at Chatham Hall often translates into special recognition, so the Rabies Club held sway for the remainder of the year. So much for adversity!

There were some experimental changes that first year of Dr. Yardley's tenure that would profoundly affect student life. Seniors now received one weekend privilege a year for "an approved reason," thereby allowing a student to leave campus without a school chaperone. Although the experiment was called "self-government," the concept was really one of individual freedom for seniors. Prior to 1949, girls had been classified according to academic performance. Those with the highest academic standing were given carte blanche in determining where they would study. All others were relegated to certain prescribed areas. No longer classified, seniors were now entirely responsible for their own behavior, giving them a freedom they had not previously enjoyed.

Essentially, Chatham Hall entered the postwar educational period as the same school it had been before the war. Fundamentally, secondary education for women should, as Dr. Yardley noted in the fall of 1950, "develop the intellect to the highest degree." In his estimation, the best education for a woman would be toward making a "superior sort of woman" rather than "an inferior sort of man." Girls in coeducational schools were receiving the same sort of education that had enabled men to "make a mess of things" in the past. For Yardley, women could make a unique contribution because of their "insight" and "tender compassion" and excel in what he vaguely called "subtler" fields where men could only follow. Subtler fields apparently did not include the practical applications of science. Instead, Yardley saw a need for artistic education and the freeing of women from what he called a "snobbery" that dictated that creativity was masculine. A school that neglected the aesthetic development of girls would be "falling down badly." The best education for young women would be within the framework of Christian living. For Yardley, secular education erred in implying that things of the spirit did not matter, and he believed that "indifference to religion is worse than no religion at all." With a grounding in good arts and sciences, young women would be able to meet the challenges of "companionship and of family living."

The art studio occupied the entire end of the third floor of Pruden Hall. It was moved to Holt Hall.

Postwar inflation was making it difficult for the families that had traditionally sent their daughters for a boarding school education. The emerging problem was the appeal of a school that was exclusively for young women. A new urgency emerged demanding that boarding schools would have to appeal to a broader spectrum of families in order to survive. The issue would be one that continually simmered for the first years of Dr. Yardley's tenure. In the early 1950s, Dr. Yardley merely praised the practicalities of academic training. Training in a modern foreign language, for example, would "lift the mind from the limitations of one's neighborhood and culture." Training in Latin, what Yardley called a "magnificent language," provided both a basis for the study of English and an entrée to a "vital" literature.

Even with such a high-minded endorsement of a rigorous academic program, the central issue in the mid-1950s was the practicality of an all-girls school education, especially considering the fact that the typical Chatham Hall graduate was married within four to eight years of her leaving Chatham Hall. "Would you give her a course of definite instructions," Yardley groused, in such matters as hygiene, childhood education, psychology and domestic science, or "out of pity" give her a round of country club–style parties laced with some business skills she could use to support herself until she headed for "the stove, the sink, and the diaper bucket?" Yardley rejected any curriculum that would either give only practical training or fun combined with job training, opting instead for what he noted was a classical curriculum of highly intensive courses in literature, mathematics, history, science and languages. All other forms of education were "soft." Soft education, Yardley noted, makes soft people. Too much fun makes them "discontented and restless." For the Chatham Hall graduate in the mid-1950s, it was not a mater of a career after graduation; it was a question of what to do with one's life before children or after children or, even more pointedly, what to do if one actually wanted a career.

Questions of money began to rival the importance of curriculum during the 1950s. Edmund Lee had turned to a wider constituency for the school first to build the chapel and later to establish the Fund for Chatham Hall following the war. While the fund had been successful in raising $150,000, the cost of its objective soared beyond the amount raised. The handsome classroom building to be called Lee Hall was never built. Instead, the board of trustees approved the construction of a library building in 1953 that would be erected in a grove of trees adjacent to the Rectory and opposite from the chapel. This would be known as the Edmund J. and Lucy Lee Library. Had the classroom building been built, a library would have been one of its features. Working with limited dollars, the New York architectural firm of Moore and Hutchins tried to solve the problem of matching the handsome colonial buildings. The task was daunting. Three structures were being considered: a library, a science building and a new dining room. Yardley underscored a growing financial problem in a school that depended largely on income from tuition and special gifts for its building program. Flatly, Chatham Hall could no longer build buildings of the "mass or design" of either Pruden or Dabney. The task for Moore and Hutchins was to design buildings that would neither clash nor detract.

While Chatham Hall was a "full school" with over 160 students enrolled, there were still financial difficulties, though of a more subtle kind than

The old library in Pruden Hall is now the Large Drawing Room.

Edmund Lee had faced in 1928. The Campaign for Chatham Hall had been a lesson in fundraising, especially as it was unable to accomplish its intended purpose by the time its limited goal had been reached. By 1953, it cost approximately $2,000 to send a girl to Chatham Hall. The tuition of $1,800, along with fees that added another $200, covered the daily operation, but inflation had made the annual income inadequate for major purchases, let alone any kind of building or renovation. Financing Chatham Hall had to become a primary focus for William Yardley. In 1953, he asked the board of trustees for permission to directly solicit donations from parents and friends, but this money was not for a specific project such as the chapel. The 1953 solicitation garnered a promising $21,822.26, but without specific reasons for the appeal, the figure fell to $15,201.47 the following year. Alumnae had already been supporting the alumnae association with dues that brought in between $1,200 and $1,300 annually. They had also annually supported an American Field Service student from Europe and were contributing to an

The proposed Edmund J. and Lucy Lee Library.

unrestricted gift fund that reached $905 in 1954. All of these efforts were brought together in the annual giving program launched in 1956.

Both David Gilmore, president of the board of trustees, and William Yardley addressed the need of Chatham Hall in two letters published in the fall 1956 edition of the *Chat*. Tuition had been raised enough to enable the school to meet daily expenses, but without a large endowment, an annual fund was the only way to make improvements. While Gilmore wrote of the concept, calling on alumnae and parents to be "as generous as their respective circumstances permit," Dr. Yardley addressed the practical needs. Highest on the list was staff salaries. The preceding school year, 1954–55, Chatham Hall had paid $168,192 in salaries to administration, faculty and support staff, more than double the 1941–42 figure of $82,015.

Participation in a pension program had doubled. Chatham Hall had begun contributing to Social Security. Now wages and retirement claimed 49 percent of the school's daily operating budget, opposed to 38 percent just ten years earlier.

Everything was more expensive. Food now cost $51,000 annually, compared to $31,000 in 1942, but here the percentage of the annual budget was about the same. Something would have to be done if Chatham Hall was to keep the tuition attractive enough so that it would not become a school exclusively for the rich. Even with the help from an annual fundraising, tuition had to be increased $600, now $1,800 compared to $1,200 in 1942, a whopping 50 percent increase.

William Yardley also included in his wish list money for scholarships. To his mind, a whole class of families had been "inflated" out of the boarding school clientele. The families of clergy and educators that depended on salary, for example, could no longer consider Chatham Hall. Sadly, even many of the alumnae could no longer afford to send a daughter to Chatham Hall. Yardley also listed funds to repair and modernize, along with some monies to be set aside for new dormitory space and a larger dining room. "Replacing plumbing is not Romantic," Yardley wrote, but a system of repair is essential. His appeal listed those things his ten-year plan would buy by 1965. The range demonstrates a commitment both to academic support and the renovation of an aging infrastructure, right down to new desks for the study hall at thirty dollars a piece.

Chapter 13

Money Matters

By 1956, the rector was, indeed, changing the school. Most significant among the changes was faculty housing. From the outset in 1894, teachers had lived in the dormitories adjacent to students. While there were housemothers, called "matrons" at first, the faculty presence was a stabilizing force, but it afforded no privacy. There had been some movement away from the dormitory under Dr. Lee, but with the exception of the Deanery for Dean Holt, the Faculty Cottage at the foot of the garden and the Mite Box next to the chapel, faculty members could expect to live in an apartment in the dorms, most often sharing bath facilities with students. A note in the faculty handbook urging teachers to bring some kind of personal decoration for their room to remind them of home suggests that many of Chatham Hall's teachers would remain single throughout their lives and return to the family home after Chatham Hall. Following the war, such facilities and such a cloistered life were no longer attractive. Housing faculty in dorms shut out the possibility of hiring male teachers. Yardley wanted his teaching faculty living in cottages where they could have privacy. Housemothers would take care of the dormitories.

The first of these cottages was given by Mr. Theodore Patterson of Cambridge, Massachusetts, to honor his daughter Marty (CH 1957). The architectural firm of Moore and Hutchins designed a simple duplex that provided two teachers with a living room, bedroom, bath and small kitchen. That same year, the small farm office that had been built in 1948 was turned into another faculty residence.

In January 1956, Dr. Edmund Lee returned to St. Mary's Chapel to assist in the ordination of Dr. William Yardley. With the head of the school again an ordained Episcopal priest, Chatham Hall fulfilled the directive of its original charter. Realizing his promise made to Edmund Lee in 1949, William Yardley once again combined the academic and spiritual leadership of the school. William Yardley was principal of the school and rector of its chapel with its parish within a parish. But Chatham Hall could not remain the school it had been under Dr. Lee. Changes in boarding school admissions were already buffeting Chatham Hall.

Where the admission process had been a more personal matter during the 1930s and '40s, with Dr. and Mrs. Lee interviewing applicants at locations in several northeastern cities as well as some other selected areas, girls now began to visit the campus with their families. By the mid-1950s, William Yardley noted that he was spending more time interviewing girls that did not attend Chatham Hall than those who would eventually matriculate. With a changing economy and the shift toward coeducation among the older New England men's boarding schools, the former dominance of girls from northeastern states shifted dramatically. By 1956, only 13 percent of the school was from New England, while 39 percent of the girls were from the South and 17 percent from the Midwest.

A cooperative effort by the National Council of Independent Schools helped boarding schools as well as other independent schools reach a wider public than these private schools had before. These would be students for whom boarding school was not a family tradition. The lure was a quality education that prepared a student for college admission, and so college preparation became an engine that drove the curriculum. When Dean Virginia Holt arrived in 1933, it had been the exceptional girl who went on to a university-level education from Chatham Hall. By the mid-1950s, it was the exceptional girl who did *not*. Colleges had also altered their pattern of admission by accepting greater percentages of students from public schools with a corresponding smaller percentage of preparatory school applicants. Combined with a conscious effort on the part of colleges to spread their enrollments over the country for a greater diversity, Chatham Hall girls could no longer count on groups of seniors being courted by prestigious colleges.

"When a daughter fails of admission to the college which her parents view as ideal," Yardley observed, "both the school and the student are blamed." Taking the college board examinations at Woodberry Forest School was an event of the past. Dean Holt had accompanied college applicants to Orange, where they had stayed a week in the school's infirmary building while attending preparatory classes before taking the battery of examinations with the boys. Now the College Board examinations were given at Chatham Hall.

In 1958, the Chatham Hall faculty thoroughly studied the curriculum with a view toward bringing it into line with university expectations and preparation for college entrance tests. A seventh period was added to the day to accommodate the new requirements. Each major course had its own additional meeting time that teachers were to use at their discretion either for make-up work, tutoring or enrichment. Ninth- and tenth-grade students added a class to their curriculum, now taking five major courses and one "minor" or elective. Eleventh and twelfth graders carried a minimum of four major and one minor course. Spanish was dropped from the curriculum in favor of concentrating on French, German or Russian. A new rotating schedule enabled classes to meet at different times throughout the week.

By the time William Yardley celebrated his tenth anniversary as rector, the United States was in a frenzy over education. The Soviet Union's launching of a successful earth-orbiting satellite and subsequent failures in the American space mission had fired new interest in education. To compete with the new national emphasis on education, Chatham Hall would have to increase its budget. But while the numbers of alumnae contributing to the new Annual Fund had increased from 25.2 percent in 1955–56 to 36.6 percent in 1958–59, the size of the average gift had dropped from a high of $33.92 to a low of $14.92. Yardley searched for ways to redirect the demands for spending. A staff of waiters still served all meals in the dining room, a labor-intensive luxury. The fact that the area was in what Yardley termed a "low labor cost pocket" had made this possible since the school's founding, but Yardley saw that a growing economy and the civil rights movement were forces that would change the school's labor situation. The building of a single factory in the area, he noted, would "change Chatham Hall from a benevolent old plantation economy." The dynamics of the economy were changing. The civil rights movement was a consideration in the economic picture. Calling the civil rights movement "troublesome times in the South," Yardley said, "Common sense and self preservation suggest that the school should prepare for a domestic revolution, whether homegrown or thrust upon us by circumstances."

Expensive labor would soon doom the wait service at meals, laundry service, maid service in dormitories and both the dairy and the farm. More pressing was the need for higher salaries for teachers and staff. Boarding schools were no longer an attractive option when it meant making personal sacrifices. For William Yardley, earlier teachers had been "a sort of governess content with other people's leavings." Chatham Hall teachers could no longer simply have a room in Pruden Hall and share in meals with students. It was essential that teachers be hired as professional educators, adequately paid, appropriately housed and accorded the dignity of a profession. By the spring of 1960, the *Chat* hinted at some of the plans that were emerging from a new visioning committee of the board of trustees. Chatham Hall would become increasingly academic with new courses such as Math V, Physics, English V and a selection of what were termed "desirables," such as German III, Asian History, Physical Geography and Chinese. By adding "Advanced Standing Courses" and teaching a "five-year" course in four years, Chatham Hall would need a larger faculty, as well as additional support staff. To accomplish this, the school would need to grow beyond the then current enrollment of 163.

By 1960, Chatham Hall had evolved into a noted college preparatory school. The home economics and secretarial courses of the 1930s had yielded to the more rigid academic curriculum. Still, the old traditions remained. Commencement that spring began as it had with few deviations for over seventy years. The Athletic Banquet in the dining room was followed later by a class song contest in the Willis Hall auditorium, where each class performed a song of its own composition. Sunday was "Class Day" beginning with the morning baccalaureate service. Seniors and their guests enjoyed box lunches of fried chicken under the great meadow oak following the service. Later that afternoon, the seniors and other classes gathered before the steps of Pruden Hall, where the editor of the yearbook, along with the president of the senior class presented the rector with the yearbook before the reading of the class will and prophecy. A buffet supper for seniors and their guests at the Rectory preceded the final vesper service in St. Mary's Chapel, and as darkness fell, seniors carried their lanterns out onto the front campus, where they turned the school over to the juniors by handing them their lanterns. Graduation on Tuesday morning in the Willis Hall auditorium brought it all to a close. Later, graduation would move to the front lawn. In all, graduation was the fulfillment of the Rectory sign with its senior in academic regalia, the junior holding the lantern of leadership, the sophomore draped in a daisy chain and the freshman carrying a daisy. Chatham Hall was its own snug little world. That same year, the school had even moved to strengthen its citadel on the hill by purchasing an old filling station on Halifax Road at the southern boundary of the campus, "where more than tanks of automobiles were filled," Yardley said, suggesting bootleg liquor operations, and a strip of land along Peach Street that controlled the entrance to the school.

The daisy chain was an important part of the graduation ceremony on the lawn in front of Pruden Hall. Girls formed the class year with the chain.

In the spring 1961 issue of *Chat*, William Yardley had warned alumnae that a good boarding school was an expensive proposition. That year, annual giving reached $50,139, a dramatic 20 percent increase over the previous year. The last of Chatham Hall's remaining indebtedness, including the money that had been borrowed for the sprinkler system and a few remaining bonds "almost as old as the school," had been wiped out. With an endowment of $200,000, the board of trustees prepared to launch a campaign that would help Chatham Hall define its role as a college preparatory school for young women. This campaign would be formally launched in 1962 seeking to raise a minimum of $845,000 to build a new dining/dormitory/infirmary wing connected to the north end of Pruden Hall. It also included a two-story arts and sciences building at the rear of Dabney, which would house three distinct laboratories, including one for a new physics course. As that building would necessitate tearing down the old Brush House, a new Brush House would be built adding even more out-of-dormitory faculty housing. A large art studio on the upper level of the new arts and sciences building would enable the school to convert the old art studio on the third floor of Pruden Hall into dormitory space. The new dining room addition would house an additional twenty-six girls on its second floor. The brochure sent to potential donors promised that Chatham Hall would set an enrollment limit of 190 to 195 girls, 20 beyond the current student body. Any more would limit "opportunities for friendship and individual instruction."

Architect's rendering of the proposed Holt Science Building.

Architect's rendering of the proposed Yardley dining room and dormitory.

Unlike the campaign to contruct a new classroom building at the end of World War II, response to the 1962 campaign was so heartening that the goal was increased to $1.3 million after its first year, and the school was within $161,000 of reaching that expanded goal by Christmas 1963.

Construction began promptly on the new Brush House and moved quickly enough that William Yardley could announce that he hoped it would be completed by the end of the summer. Its design was reminiscent of the Faculty Cottage built by Dr. Lee in that it would provide housing for four teachers. However, the Faculty Cottage had been built as four bedrooms sharing a common living room, with two bedrooms sharing a bath. The new Brush House was built in two pavilions connected by a commons area, but each apartment had its own bath, kitchen and living area. As such, the accommodations were more like apartment-style residences, reflecting the school's new attempt to attract both male and female teachers. The roof was up on Virginia Holt Hall, the new arts and sciences building, by winter of 1963, but the new dining room/dormitory progressed more slowly. Together, the new buildings were what William Yardley called "handsome and well-proportioned," neither a "pallid colonial reproduction." Holt Hall

Interior of the new Lee Library, 1954.

would house "exactly the right facilities for a modern program in the arts and sciences."

At the opening of the 1963–64 session, even the dining room/dormitory wing was mostly complete. Half again larger than the old dining room, the new dining room was distinguished by a large bay window and a spacious foyer decorated with antiques. The most distinguished of the antiques was a Philadelphia grandfather's clock crafted before 1790 by Benjamin Reeve. With two new buildings on campus, it was suddenly evident that the changes were dramatic. Dormitory rooms had to be renumbered to accommodate the thirteen new dorm rooms. The infirmary had been relocated to the first floor of Pruden Hall in a health suite that occupied half of the former dining room and the entire old kitchen. A nurse's apartment, reception room, examining room and six semiprivate bedrooms were directly across a new hallway from a new administrative office and the new alumnae office. Not only could students now walk the entire length of Pruden Hall in a first-floor hallway, but they could also get from one end of Dabney Hall's lower level in another new hall. With the construction of the new arts and sciences building, a corridor was cut through the old chemistry room under the study hall, leaving a place for two student lounges on one side and "Women's World," a coin-operated laundry, on the other. At the opposite end of the hall, the room nearest to the chapel was converted into a language laboratory with listening and recording capabilities. Upstairs in Pruden and Dabney Halls, the old teacher accommodations were now little apartments with their own sitting rooms, bedrooms and baths. Immediately, the most interesting and most favored of these apartments occupied the space that had been the former art studio.

Chapter 14

Open to the World

With the construction of bypasses around towns along the U.S. 29 corridor, including a Chatham bypass, the outside world could now get to Chatham more easily. One bonus was Fathers' Weekend. This began in 1961 as a means to enable fathers to learn more about their daughters' school. Fathers attended classes, picnicked under the great oak and attended chapel. That first father/daughter dance the Saturday evening of the first Fathers' Weekend was the first time a Chatham Hall girl was allowed to kiss her date goodnight.

The world had not yet changed a great deal at Chatham Hall. In many ways, the school's rigid codes had not changed much in seventy-five years. With a view toward legislating "fair play" and protecting against "thoughtlessness," a plethora of rules governed what the student handbook of 1964 called "the business of group living." Limiting each girl to two framed pictures and not more than four photographs ensured the orderliness of rooms. A small pillow and one stuffed animal personalized each girl's bed. Dress reflected the "ideal of simplicity" outlined in a special code entitled "Dress Regulations." Students were expected to wear skirts and blouses to class, but they had to change into something more attractive for dinner. Socks were reserved for the athletic field; stockings were appropriate for all other occasions. Students were also expected to dress "carefully" for chapel, Saturday evening entertainments in Willis Hall or when going to town. Moccasin shoes or loafers were considered "contraband." Lipstick was discouraged but permitted for dinner and all day Sunday and Monday.

Students were assigned to a table with a faculty member as hostess in the Pruden Hall dining room. Stewards helped bring food to the tables.

Colored fingernail polish was forbidden; dyed hair and elaborate hairdos were discouraged as being "in dubious taste." Casual wear was restricted to dormitory levels, but dressing gowns and slippers had to be worn when going to shower.

The weekend began after regular classes on Saturday with an entertainment that evening in Willis Hall and extended into Monday. There were few chances to get off campus other than a walk into Chatham to see a movie at the Chatham Theater on Pruden Street. Leaving campus was permitted if accompanying a parent to lunch on Sunday or Monday, and then only one meal per weekend. Any girl going out for Sunday dinner with her parents had to return for the Service League meeting that evening. Seniors could take three weekend leaves from school, but only two of these could include the whole of Saturday. Juniors were permitted two weekends, sophomores one weekend and freshmen one overnight per semester.

With students on college campuses demanding more of a voice in eliminating what they saw as archaic rules, it was inevitable that the same demand for representation to affect change would filter down to high schools, including Chatham Hall. The first evidence of an emerging change at Chatham Hall came with the establishment of the senate. There had been a student council since 1918, but it had evolved into the organization that was charged with maintaining discipline and a high sense of personal honor. The honor code had evolved during Dr. Lee's tenure as rector into what the student handbook termed "Christianity in action." "All actions," it stated, "are under God's judgment"; each member of the community was responsible for those actions to herself, the community and to God.

There were five main principles to the honor code. The first of these principles was honor, interpreted as a girl's personal integrity of truthfulness and respect for the rights and property of others. The second principle was loyalty, meaning a girl's loyalty to the ideals of Chatham Hall. The third principle, reverence, applied to a girl's conduct in the chapel as well as suggesting that she cultivate personal humility. Responsibility, the fourth principle, specified a girl's attentiveness to duties, rules and citizenship. The final principle, order, not only related to order and cleanliness of a room but also respect for school property. Even this interpretation of the honor code was confusingly rigid. The student council was not a forum for addressing changes to it or any other school rule.

The first forum for affecting change came when students gathered on April 16, 1963, to found the senate as an alternative to the seniors-only student council. The senate was never intended to detract from the authority of the ten-member student council. Instead, the senate's purpose was to act as a more representative forum for discussing school problems, offering solutions and shouldering community responsibilities. Representation was a problem from the outset. Initially, the membership comprised the president and nine other members of the student council, the president of the Service League, the president and vice-president of each of the four classes, the president of the day students, the rector, the dean of students, the dean of the faculty, the faculty sponsor of the Service League and two resident representatives of the faculty. Three new members from each class were added later. These and the faculty representatives served from January to January in an attempt at continuity.

The first issues addressed went straight to the heart of the rigid rules governing earrings, lipstick, eye makeup and hair dying. Freshmen were the first to gain an additional overnight, although limited to a 150-mile radius of the school. Another victory was the abolition of the compulsory rest hour every Sunday from 2:00 p.m. until 3:00.

With changing attitudes toward student involvement in governance, several other matters in the mid-1960s changed Chatham Hall. An anonymous gift in 1964 led to the development of a campus behind Pruden and Dabney Halls that extended from the old powerhouse to the new Virginia Holt Hall. The area was intended as a green lawn rather than an extension of the old formal garden that remained behind the long arcade. Workmen tore up the road that had once extended along the back of the buildings, leaving its truncated ends to service a loading dock behind each of the main buildings. St. Mary's Chapel finally gained an organ to replace the "temporary" movie house organ that had been patched together before World War II. While chapel services "made do" with the electric organ brought over from Willis Hall, electronic organ music was not suitable for St. Mary's. When a tracker organ built by Orgelbauermeister Detlef Klüker of Brackwede, Germany, was placed in the choir loft of the chapel, it opened new space in the chancel for seating. This was paneled in with seats, cornice, miniature pilasters and columns to match the rest of the paneling from 1940.

By 1966, Chatham Hall reached its largest enrollment: 199, only 10 of whom were day students. Of this number, 20 were freshmen, 61 sophomores, 65 juniors and 53 seniors. They came largely from the South and Midwest, the two regions accounting for 56 percent of the student body. With the exception of 10 percent representing such exotic areas as the Far West, Southwest and foreign countries, the other large group came from Mid-Atlantic states. The New England representation had dropped to 13 percent. Two deans who taught part-time joined twenty-seven full-time faculty members and three full-time physical education instructors. In addition, there was a business manager, a bursar, an assistant bursar, three housemothers, two nurses, a librarian and one assistant, nine office staff and two doctors on call. Nine families lived on campus, with ten children between the ages of one and thirteen. One other child was away at boarding school, and two were attending college. Tuition, room and board was $3,000; 20 students shared $26,800 in scholarship money. Only the American Field Service student received a full scholarship. Of the graduating class, 95 percent went off to college, 80 percent of them to a four-year college and the remainder to junior colleges. For the first time in Chatham Hall's history, more seniors selected a coed college than a woman's college.

Chapter 15

Remaining Single-Sex

Nationally, there had been a growing drumbeat for single-sex institutions to become coeducational. William Yardley raised the issue for Chatham Hall in the spring 1969 issue of the alumnae newsmagazine. The national issue of cooperation, coordination or coeducation and even merging a boys' school with a girls' school would be tested when twenty-six seniors and juniors from both Chatham Hall and Woodberry Forest exchanged schools. The boys first traveled to Chatham and lived in the rooms over the dining room for a week; the girls returned with them to Orange for the second week of the exchange. In explaining the experiment to the alumnae, Dr. Yardley noted that girls between the seventh and tenth grades were physically stronger, taller, more intellectual and more mature than boys the same age, but by the eleventh grade, boys had, in general, caught up. An exchange in those years would prepare girls heading toward the coed colleges. That recent phenomenon called for "special preparation." Yardley wrote, "I am inclined to think that the boys of Woodberry did more in their one week of gentle treatment to prepare our seniors for life in college than the school has done in the other thirty-two weeks of the academic year."

The exchange underscored the possible benefits of "harmonizing" the schools' curricula with a view toward eliminating those courses that were either expensive or redundant.

Still, no one in either school wanted to drop cherished traditions or lose identity, so any movement toward a trimester-long exchange would have to be approached with what Yardley termed "great caution." Tara Stack, one of the seniors participating in the exchange, wrote for the *Chat* praising the benefits of coeducation, especially a social life that was "more normal" since social activities did not have to be crammed into two to three weekends a year, a circumstance that made things get "drastically out of proportion" at Chatham Hall.

Coeducation was again the major topic addressed by the following *Chat* six months after the exchange with Woodberry Forest. An article by Dexter M. Keezer reprinted from the *New Republic* referred to the push for coeducation as a desire for "proximity" driven by an instinct for institutional survival. For Keezer, the result was what he called "shortchanging" in institutions that had become coeducational. His advice supported Chatham Hall's remaining single-sex. By "holding on and staying lean," single-sex institutions would ultimately secure a better level of education for women in the United States and, in his opinion, "a more exalted role for women in shaping the culture of the nation."

That same issue of the *Chat* included a sobering profile of students that differed markedly from those of an earlier generation. Yardley commented

Music Club, 1971.

that students faced a new reality in the nuclear arms race coupled with the threatening Cold War. To him, students in 1969 were no longer able to count on a full life span. Nor was there respect for government or rituals. "The young," Yardley noted, "live in a strangely different and frightening frame of reference." If their world could be blotted out in an instant, what was the use of preparing for a future? For many, Christianity was a superstition and government was not honest. With a limited life, a person was responsible only to herself, and hedonistic pleasure at least made the uncertainty easier to handle. Two fully stocked fall-out shelters under the library stood as mute testimony of this resignation.

Perhaps most frightening of all was the notion of what Yardley called "the wisdom of youth." Age had become "stupid by an accumulation of experience"; it had failed to evaluate and make useful. The upshot of this social change was that students had started to demand change in their schools. Yardley was hopeful that Chatham Hall would avoid confrontation by having faculty and staff work on their relationships with students.

Changing student attitudes toward such issues as coeducation caught the attention of the alumnae. Dr. Yardley's initial portrait of the changing student was further defined specifically in terms of Chatham Hall. For Dr. Yardley, the Chatham Hall girl of 1970 was generally more independent and better prepared than her predecessors and less willing to accept things on faith. While the typical Chatham Hall girl continued to seek recognition by her peers, the companionship of a group and the desire to serve, she also wanted to participate in decision making. This was not just wanting a "piece of the action" but wanting to be part of the process determining what that action would be. The senate had been formed in response to the call for wider representation. A similar response to student suggestions is also evident in a new Senior Independent Project program that had begun modestly in the spring of 1969, the year Chatham Hall accepted its first four African American students.

The senior project program grew instantly, involving 95 percent of the senior class by the spring of 1970. It was intended to give seniors an opportunity to explore independently a field of interest apart from their structured curriculum, as well as provide a means to relate to a rapidly changing world. The program called for seniors to be away from campus almost the entire month of May, returning in time for graduation. Those with more local projects left the campus at 8:00 a.m., returning by dinner. Independence was key to the entire venture.

The same issue of the *Chat* that described the senior project program contained some troubling admissions news. A changing pattern in

Language Lab.

Indoor athletics were held in Willis Hall until construction of the gym. Otherwise, girls were ferried to Chatham's armory. Volleyball in Willis was a challenge.

applications showed numbers dropping off, especially from the North and the East. Dr. Yardley blamed economic conditions, in part, but also noted that coeducational schools were suffering less. Boarding schools in general were suffering the greatest drop in enrollment. Not wanting to "scrape up girls,"

Yardley enlisted the aid of alumnae in deepening the pool of applicants so that the school could continue to be selective. Chatham Hall was not alone. Economic conditions, coeducation and a general drop in interest in boarding education during the 1970s plagued other schools as well.

In asking alumnae to help identify prospective students, Dr. Yardley defined the student who would be attracted to Chatham Hall. She would love country life, be scholarly by nature, enjoy the challenge of good work and enjoy the immersion into a small-school community. One further quality suggested that a candidate for Chatham Hall would be expected to renounce the growing national trend toward student activism. A prospective Chatham Hall girl should not oppose "stretching out her girlhood at the expense of somewhat premature adulthood."

With one more exchange experiment, this time with Brooks Academy in Massachusetts, William Yardley announced that he would retire on June 30, 1971, making him one of the three long-tenured heads of the school: eighteen years for Elizabeth May Willis, twenty-one years for Edmund Jennings Lee and twenty-two years for William Woolsey Yardley. Together, these three had governed the school for sixty-one years of its seventy-one-year history.

Chapter 16

A Period of Stress

While the shifting attitudes of popular culture challenged Chatham Hall during the 1970s, there were other sinister forces that were even more threatening. By the 1974–75 academic year, America's annual 8.5 percent inflation spiral, the oil embargo of 1973 and 1974 and a steadily weakening economy had finally ushered in a severe recession. A crippled economy exacerbated the declining applicant pool that had already been weakened by a shrinking student population.

All boarding schools were trying to cope with enormous problems. First, they were competing for the same students from a dwindling pool of applicants. Second, these students were frequently ones for whom the boarding tradition was new. Third, the changing culture on college campuses that included recreational drugs had filtered down to secondary schools, presenting a whole new array of challenges for boarding schools. On top of all this, inflation ate away at endowments, escalated the cost of educating and wrecked budgets. In the spring of 1975, Anne Bryant (CH 1967) reported as a member of the Chatham Hall Long Range Planning Committee that schools in general were "beset with problems." With enrollment down "across the board," she appealed to all alumnae. Citing the strength each woman had gained by "sharing" two to four years with the school, Anne Bryant called on her fellow alumnae to "help Chatham Hall through this period of stress."

When the board of trustees appointed the Reverend William Reeves to replace William Yardley, it confirmed the tradition begun with Dr. Lee that the head of the school should be an Episcopal clergyman. As rector, William Reeves sought to sustain Chatham Hall's commitment to single-sex education, even after a second student exchange with Woodberry Forest in the fall of 1975 again displayed the economic lure of combining operations. His efforts to solve the other stresses were also successful, but even with a stemming of the downward trend in enrollment, the obstacles finally overwhelmed both the rector and the board of trustees by the end of 1975, moving Reverend Reeves to resign before the conclusion of the school year.

The Reverend William Reeves.

With the abrupt resignation of William Reeves, leadership of Chatham Hall fell to the Reverend Russell Ingersoll, the academic dean who had just taken office the previous September. Clearly, Chatham Hall was reeling from the sudden resignation and was facing the New Year with what Ingersoll called "emotions of shock, grief, loss, and bewilderment." Now, nearly fifty years after the crisis in finances and enrollment that had brought Edmund Lee to Chatham Hall, Russell Ingersoll, too, faced an immediate need to reduce costs enough to balance the budget in a time of ballooning inflation. The trick was to successfully compete with a variety of day schools and newly coeducational boarding schools, most of which offered more lavish facilities.

The times were dangerous. Other single-sex boarding schools had solved their admissions shortfalls by turning to coeducation, thereby instantly doubling their candidate pool. Yielding to the tide of campus unrest, other church schools had turned toward a more secular, humanistic education. The legacy of Reeve's leadership was that Chatham Hall remained "self-consciously Christian," a legacy Russell Ingersoll saw as probably the most "profound…any headmaster

The Reverend Russell Ingersoll.

of a church school could leave." Equally important was that Chatham Hall remained true to its original purpose to educate young women. As long as Chatham Hall continued to develop its facilities and shape its curriculum to meet the emerging needs of young women, the challenge of being an all-girls boarding school would be the greatest opportunity rather than a liability.

Russell Ingersoll remained acting head of the school throughout the spring and fall of 1976 while the board of trustees interviewed other candidates for the position of new rector. Although some apprehension remained, there was also a sense of new beginnings that brought with it renewed confidence that the downward trend in both finances and admissions could be reversed. Even an anonymous gift of a new station wagon and a new mower for the campus was enough to spark a comment in *Chat* that suddenly "nothing seemed impossible." Enrollment was large enough for the 1976–77 academic year that the dorm rooms in Yardley could be reopened.

In December 1976, Dr. Robert Pugh, president of the board of trustees, announced to the faculty that Russell Ingersoll would be the new rector. News at school was good in general. There were honors seminars sponsored by the English Department; French students experimented with an immersion weekend. A new concert grand piano, a memorial to Helen Gordon Ingram (CH 1952), graced the Willis stage. All other things seemed to be "good" as well as normal, including the "Spring Open" annual dance with boys on campus for the weekend, a Little Sisters Weekend and a trip to the Peaks of Otter.

On the surface, it seemed that Chatham Hall's situation was improving. The Annual Fund continued to grow in spite of a spiraling inflation. In a way, inflation even "helped" as inflated dollars gave Chatham Hall an opportunity to reduce its deficit from 1976 through 1978. But outside the calm of southern Virginia, there was a steady underlying drumbeat in the education community that throbbed with the need for radical change. By 1978, the United Press International was reporting that only twenty-five all-girls' boarding schools remained in America; several of those were considering yielding to the pressure for coeducation.

With a commitment from the rector and the board of trustees to remain single-sex, Chatham Hall once again faced redefining itself within the perceived changing role of women in American society and as a school devoted expressly to the education of young women. Writing to the alumnae in the autumn 1977 *Chat*, Susannah Gould, dean of the faculty, noted that the school would have to face "new dimensions" in the education of young women. While the traditional roles of wife, mother and homemaker remained, Chatham Hall's curriculum had to prepare students for "whichever role or combination of roles she selects." Those roles and the educational response became the focus of a three-day spring 1978 symposium, "Educating Women for the 21st Century." Keynote speaker Frances T. Farenhold, president of Wells College, spoke about future directions in the education of women while also looking at new problems and challenges facing women in America.

President Farenhold's address sparked two in-house studies. Students gathered to study their own needs while all academic departments examined their own purposes as well as curriculum with a special regard to student needs and college requirements. With consultants from the School of Education of Virginia Commonwealth University, Cornell and the National Association of Independent Schools, a faculty committee first reexamined the school's philosophy as stated in the 1970 Southern Asssociation of Colleges and Schools Self-Study and then rewrote the curriculum, changing requirements and expectations.

Rather than being sweeping, the changes added a little but largely confirmed what had been required since Richard Willis had established the basic curriculum in 1898: four years of English, three of mathematics, three of history and three of a single language. New to the curriculum was the requirement that girls take two years of laboratory science in addition to an introductory general science course. Holding to the school's tradition, girls were still required to take one year of religion, one year of either fine or performing arts and a semester of health. Important to the curriculum was the retention of physical education in each semester of a girl's tenure at Chatham Hall.

New weaving looms and potter's wheels added a dimension to the art program that would hopefully appeal to girls. New events strengthened the

Old farm buildings near the stables became part of the art program in the 1970s.

social aspect of the school. One Saturday in January 1978, the entire school decked out in Elizabethan finery for a day-long "royal festival." Riders jousted, dancers performed Elizabethan dances and the entire school, students and faculty, paid homage to the queen, played by Mrs. Connie Gibson, the dean of students. Chatham Hall turned to a celebration of its most noted alumna with a mini exhibit of Georgia O'Keeffe's watercolor *Pansies*, done in 1904 and given to classmate Susan Young Wilson. Reproductions of O'Keeffe's 1905 yearbook illustrations complemented the watercolor.

Even with a positive outlook, there were problems that threatened to overwhelm the school. A succession of years when new girls outnumbered the old girls tended to weaken allegiance to traditions. Older faculty, who had been in service to Chatham Hall since former, calmer times, refused to believe that "their girls" could possibly yield to drugs and alcohol as had students in other schools. The truth was that Chatham Hall could not remain an island in the turbulent sea of the 1970s. Drug and alcohol use among teens had become such a national issue that Chatham Hall adopted its first comprehensive drug policy, presenting it to students and sending it to parents.

There were violations of the drug policy. Rector Russell Ingersoll attempted to control the damage by employing draconian measures. New younger house parents stayed up at night patrolling the halls and stairwells to thwart any possible activity. Even if it meant reducing the student body by a significant percentage, Ingersoll was determined to save the school from the influence of drugs. The board of trustees agreed with the sentiment but disagreed with the methods. After losing the confidence of the board of trustees, Russell Ingersoll, like Reverend Reeves, left Chatham Hall, but this time leaving its leadership first to the board and then to an interim headmaster.

Certainly, the students knew that what the rector had attempted had been the right thing to do. The 1979 yearbook contains a poignant tribute to the Ingersolls. In a piece titled "L'Envoi," the seniors confessed that they had hurt the rector "sometimes more than we intended." Their lesson was one that was hardly new; rather it was one that had been repeated throughout the history of Chatham Hall when students finally understood the devotion of their teachers. Their simple admission: "But now, as you leave us, we come to know that you loved us more than we realized." Its concluding affirmation was a blessing: "God bless you and your family."

Chapter 17

Take a Deep Breath

There was something prophetic about the deaths of Anne Csaszar and "Pete" Taylor during 1979. The two had been a part of William Yardley's school that had flourished during the 1950s and '60s. But the students of the 1970s were markedly different, some even scornful of the old status quo. It was time to reflect and reevaluate. Enrollment was down. Money was so tight that logging of the old-growth forest near the cherished meadow oak was permitted in order to balance the budget. Other schools yielded to coeducation and mergers to deepen their pools of applicants and coordinate budgets.

Mr. Donald Hagerman accepted the position of interim headmaster to give the trustees ample time to find a new head for the school. In June 1980, his letter to alumnae stated that he was "relieved" to report that a "change for the better" was clearly evident. "While the effect of the 'drug culture' has not lessened perceptibly," he wrote, "it is my strong feeling that the younger members of our society are recognizing the errorrs in judgment."

The two years of Hagerman's headship were good for Chatham Hall. There was a universal relief that the school was not only stable but was also striving to regain its leadership. In July 1981, the trustees announced that the school's new leader would be Jerry A. "Dutch" VanVoorhis.

Chatham Hall opened with 135 students in 1981. This was to be a year of study for "Dutch" VanVoorhis. Don Hagerman agreed to remain for one year as a special assistant to the new rector. The year is noteworthy in that it strengthened the sense of renewal. The operating deficit shrank to $55,000 during the 1981–82 school year, and the student body grew to 160. That year also brought the first of a series of large contributions that would eventually grow the endowment twelve-fold by the time the school would celebrate its first one hundred years.

Mr. Don Hagerman and his wife, Ibba.

A $1.5 million grant by the Kenan Foundation gave the endowment its first boost and the first funding for projects in more than a decade. By 1984, that grant would be matched to grow the endowment. The $500,000 enabled the school to begin projects that would enhance facilities. The first of these was to divide the Dabney study hall into six modern classrooms. One year later, the dank Dabney basement classrooms were converted into a community center with a lounge, student kitchen, viewing room and other facilities that promoted recreation and student life.

VanVoorhis also brought changes to the academic curriculum. Starting with the 1982–83 session, the year was divided into trimesters rather than semesters and classes met over what was termed a five-and-a-half-day schedule. All subjects met five times a week on a rotating schedule. Planning also began on moving the library into a renovated Willis Hall in order to have the center of research and study adjacent to the classrooms. Through such a complete overhaul of the library, Chatham Hall would become the first school of its type to have an electronic catalogue and access to information databases available from remote sources.

Mr. Jerry A. VanVoorhis.

By the fall 1985 issue of the *Chat*, Jerry VanVoorhis could report that the "renaissance" of Chatham Hall was an "accepted fact." While the number of renovation and building projects would make this "renaissance" seem to be one of bricks and mortar, the 1980s also marked a revitalization of the honor code and a revision in personal accountability with regard to discipline. When Dutch VanVoorhis first came to Chatham Hall, he commented that he was committed to secondary education because it was the place where education "actually worked." Just two years later, he sharpened his focus on boarding schools, calling them the "only true educators of character." In part, this was addressed to the substantial group that worried about changing demographics and a shrinking pool of applicants that affected admissions. For VanVoorhis, the idea of teaching character was either lost or subordinated to expedient decisions, such as coeducation, that dulled the focus on character building. Chatham Hall should stand out as the best option for a superior education for young women.

The most important part of character building was the honor code. By December 1982, a faculty-student committee had written the definition of honor that continues to stand for Chatham Hall. There had been concern that small matters of a disciplinary nature had crept into the honor code, putting a failure to check out a library book on par with stealing. The concept of honor as personal integrity was reaffirmed in the pledge not to lie, cheat or steal. The importance of not tolorating such behavior was again emphasized. The committee had written to other boarding schools to determine how they handled infractions of their codes of honor. For most, it was a faculty committee. Some schools did nothing at all when their honor codes were violated. Overall, most of the schools contacted saw an honor

The new Lee Library opened in 1987 as one of the most technologically advanced libraries in a private secondary school.

code as unworkable in modern education. The reaffirmation that each person in the Chatham Hall community would annually pledge to uphold the honor code and that the responsibility for adjudicating any infractions would be handled by an elected student council would lead Mills E. Godwin, the former governor of Virginia, to comment that he was "greatly impressed with your Honor Code and the way it operates at Chatham Hall." The fact that the whole issue of personal integrity and personal responsibility was maintained by an elected student council put Chatham Hall once again at the forefront in teaching character.

A disciplinary code was the second piece of the school's new approach to developing character. Prior to 1990, Chatham Hall girls were assigned "points" for infractions. Missing chapel, skipping a seated meal or talking during study hall earned a girl varying point values. If a girl exceeded an established number, she was confined to campus for the weekend. At a certain point, punishment became more serious. In 1990, Chatham Hall abolished the point system as being arbitrarily punitive and instead embraced the "Purple and Golden Rule," an independent reckoning based on the golden rule. Responsibility was individual, not imposed by a piece of paper. Rather than simply assigning a number of negative points, a teacher now needed to confront the girl, discuss the behavior and together conclude what the girl might do to correct herself.

There is no doubt that all boarding schools found admissions recruiting difficult during the 1980s and 1990s. Once a prospective student had visited the campus and been part of the school's experience, Chatham Hall was likely to be her choice. But a single-sex education in a remote area of Virginia was frequently a deterrant. Making sure that Chatham Hall would be the best possible choice would take an investment. Building on the success of raising the endowment and funding major renovations, Dutch VanVoorhis announced the "Commitment to Excellence" campaign in the summer of 1986. This would raise $5 million for construction and add another $1.5 million to the endowment.

In many respects, Jerry Van Voorhis was a builder. Under him, classrooms were renovated, and dorm rooms were modernized with a view toward changing demands of students. There was a new gym, the first since the Dabney gym had been converted in the 1920s, and a new dance space. The beautiul new electronic library would be a crowning achievement. But above all, there was a significant endowment. Chatham Hall was regaining its stability.

One quirky piece of history from the 1980s was the invasion by Hollywood during the spring and summer of 1989. The Governor's Film Office convinced Chatham Hall to allow Paramount Pictures to use the campus as a setting for its comedy *Crazy People*. Pruden Hall became the set for an upscale private sanitorium. The dining room of Yardley became the boardroom of a Madison Avenue advertising agency. A few students and teachers were part of scenes filmed at the beginning of the process, but when the first star, John Malkovich, was replaced by Dudley Moore, the original scenes were abandoned. The filming became part of daily life. Students would freeze and remain silent when a buzzer announced that filming was commencing. The novelty wore off, but some of the actors remained favorites. Dudley Moore would play the grand piano in the Well after dinner while students sat and listened. He even gave a formal concert in Yardley after dinner one evening. Residents of Chatham were especially interested in the filming. Daryl Hannah lived on Main Street. When John F. Kennedy Jr. visited the set, he would daily jog the streets, often followed by a group of well-coiffed women who had just taken up jogging.

With just four years until the centennial, preparations began for a celebration of the first one hundred years. Teams scoured the campus closets and attics in search of memorabilia. Old photographs, a white mortarboard

St. Mary's Chapel.

from the 1940s, class scrapbooks with programs of plays and recitals enjoyed over the years, notebooks and even some lesson plans began to surface. Dr. Lee's "magic lantern slides" of his China mission jogged memories of Dr. and Mrs. Lee. Students, alumnae and faculty collected memorabilia for a time capsule that was planted in front of Pruden Hall on Sunday, November 7, 1993. The plaque marking the spot invites the school to open the 100th anniversary time capsule on the same day in 2044.

The celebration weekend began Friday, April 22, 1994. One of the highlights was an exhibition of artwork created by alumnae that had been gathered by Laura Bradley (CH 1970). This included three works by Georgia O'Keeffe. Books authored by alumnae were exhibited by the library for the alumnae who arrived on campus for the celebration. Dinner and dancing under a huge tent pitched on the upper hockey field was the festive highlight of the weekend. The entire school—including students, attending alumnae, faculty and administrators—gathered in front of Pruden Hall for a panoramic photograph just like the one taken in the winter of 1912.

Epilogue

Sealing the Vision

In the breezes that blew through the centennial celebrations, one can imagine that there must have been the whisperings of ghosts of the past that thought it would never happen. How many times had Chatham Episcopal Institute, now Chatham Hall, come to the brink of extinction and been saved just at the darkest moment? It had been over one hundred years since C. Orlando Pruden had driven his buggy up the hill to the east of Chatham to ask the widow Gilmer to rent her home for a new school. How many dividends had the $3,000 in local donations for Pruden's new school returned? How many dark nights had plagued how many heads of the school as they tried to find a way to save it? Now entering its second century, Chatham Hall's prospects for the future had never seemed so bright.

By 1994, the "Campaign for Chatham Hall" sought to raise $17 million, in part to continue strengthening academic resources and in part to double the endowment to $25 million. The new century would mark significant achievements for the school. Jerry VanVoorhis moved on to a university position after steering the school through the years of rebuilding and restrengthening. Mrs. Marlene Shaw became the first woman to head the school since Mable Eleanor Stone left in 1928. She would also be the first to bear the title "rector." During Mrs. Shaw's five-year tenure, the Mars family donated a splendid indoor riding facility that opened during the summer of 1998. Academic requirements were increased to meet the challenge of greater global demands. There were additional requirements for foreign language and science. The gift of a science and technology center in 2002 would mark

Mrs. Marlene Rutledge Shaw.

a new emphasis on preparing girls for careers in the sciences, technology and engineering. Technology became a vital tool in expanding the school's commitment to excellence.

The challenges facing Chatham Hall and other schools were clearly financial. Of each dollar spent to educate each girl in 1998, only fifty-six cents came from tuition. The remaining forty-four cents came through other resources: twenty-two cents from annual giving, thirteen cents from endowment income and nine cents from a variety of sources. In the 1930s, Dr. Lee had been able to set aside a portion of each annual budget for a "building fund." Private resources were now necessary. Unlike the doubts of the 1960s, however, Chatham Hall now embraced its unique status as an all-girls preparatory school. Strength lies in the conviction that young women learn differently than young men. The core of a Chatham Hall education is that girls thrive when they assume leadership roles. They excel when they are guardianns of their own traditions and shapers of their own destinies.

Dr. Gary Fountain succeeded Marlene Shaw as rector in 2003. Both Dr. Fountain and his wife, Missy, strengthened the school's financial base. As an English teacher himself, Dr. Fountain rallied resources to bring an even greater sense of intellectual commitment. A new program, the Discovery Challenge, gave girls an opportunity to plan an individual research project with a faculty mentor. New classes in world cultures, economics and global issues defined an increased global awareness. Students joined faculty on language immersion studies in France and Spain. An awareness of social responsibility gained new emphasis in both a "Social Entrepreneur"

Above: Shaw Science Building under construction.

Right: Dr. Gary Fountain.

program that saw the construction of houses for Habitat for Humanity and an annual service trip to South Africa.

One of the most significant new programs under Gary Fountain is the annual visit of a world leader in residence. These have included Nobel Prize winner Shirin Ebadi, conservationist Jane Goodall, Liberian president

Ellen Johnson-Sirleaf and former president of Pakistan Benazir Bhutto. There have been others just as significant. In addition, there have been poets and other writers as well, such as Nikki Giovanni and Li-Young Lee. Each contributes to the sense that the Chatham Hall education includes a delicious exposure to a world of artistic talent, political courage and successful personal endeavor.

It has now been twenty years since Chatham Hall celebrated its first century. If the first one hundred years were a gathering of power and energy, the new century already seems to be one of confidence. Surely the $31 million bequest of Elizabeth Beckwith Nilsen (CH 1931) may seem to make that confidence easy, but it is just as much Chatham Hall's belief in education for young women, its commitment to academic excellence, its nuturing of personal integrity and its strengthening of spiritual vigor that are the driving forces. Surely, all depends on the support of those who believe in the mission of Chatham Hall, but together there is a force that will always be Chatham Hall. No one can be here for long without coming to this belief.

Esto Perpetua!

Photo by Catherine M. LaDuke.

Index

L

M

N

O

P

R

S

V

W

About the Author

William Black came to Chatham Hall in 1982 as chair of the English Department. Since that time, he has served the school as director of admission, director of the Edmund J. and Lucy Lee Library and academic dean. He now serves as the school's historian and archivist. His academic credentials include an undergraduate degree from the College of William and Mary and two graduate degrees from Duke University, a master's and a doctor of philosophy in English. He is president of the Pittsylvania Historical Society and serves the town of Chatham, Virginia, as a member of the town council. He and his wife live in Chatham with their golden retriever, Chlöe.

Photograph by Lisa Richmond (CH 1984) Photography.